The Life of
HENRY
DRUMMOND
(1851–1897)

The Life of
HENRY
DRUMMOND
(1851–1897)

THE DRUMMOND TRUST · STIRLING

This edition first published in 1997 by
THE DRUMMOND TRUST
3 Pitt Street, Stirling FK8 2EY

Original edition © George Adam Smith 1899
(published as *The Life of Henry Drummond (1851-1897)*,
Hodder & Stoughton, 1899)

This edition (edited and condensed) © The Drummond Trust, 1997

ISBN 0 9529877 0 8

British Library Cataloguing in Publication Data
A catalogue record for this book
is available from the British Library.

ISBN 0952987708

Cover and **design concept** by Mark Blackadder.
Cover photograph and **signature** taken from the original volume of *The Life of
Henry Drummond (1851-1897)* by George Adam Smith (Hodder & Stoughton, 1899).
Back cover photographs used by permission of the Revd Finlay Stewart.
Typeset in 11/13 pt Bembo.
Printed and bound by Athenaeum Press Ltd, Gateshead.

Contents

Preface

HENRY Drummond was a truly remarkable man. World-famous as both scientist and evangelist, he strove to reconcile the new theories of science with the doctrines of Christianity.

Believing that 'science has supplied theology with a theory which the intellect can accept, and which for the devout mind leaves everything more worthy of worship than before', he declared that the crown of Evolution is Christianity.

But he was also a man who profoundly affected the lives of ordinary people – not only his close friends, but men and women of all walks of life who were inspired by his preaching and his counsel. It was particularly among young people – and most of all students – that many believed that he did his greatest work.

Such a man and such a life deserve commemoration – with special appropriateness as the centenary approaches of Drummond's death on 11 March 1897.

The Drummond Trust, while tracing its origins to Peter Drummond, Henry's uncle (mentioned in Chapter 2 of this volume), has always been conscious of the great significance of Henry's work. Thus, in conjunction with the University of Stirling, the Trust hosts the biennial Drummond Lectures 'to commemorate the achievement of Henry Drummond of Stirling'.

The Trustees, in considering how to mark this centenary, approved the proposal to produce a much shortened version of the biography by George Adam Smith, which was published three years after Drummond's death. It would nowadays be described as the 'authorised biography', as the writer, besides being a close and like-minded friend who knew some of Drummond's career at first hand, had access to diaries, papers, letters both to and from Drummond, and the testimonies of many people. The original is indeed a comprehensive, authoritative and engrossing work, which in some form should be available to a modern readership.

This volume seeks to present the gist of it. George Adam Smith's text is preserved throughout, except where a transition or omission necessitates very slight alteration for the sake of continuity. Let it be clear therefore that what is here offered is not a work of new research or scholarship, but a form of re-publication of an outstanding biography, written by a man who himself later achieved distinction as Biblical scholar and parish minister, as Principal of Aberdeen University and Moderator of the General Assembly of the Church of Scotland.

The Drummond Trustees wish to express their sincere gratitude to Mrs Janet Carleton (a daughter of George Adam Smith) and other members of the family for granting permission for this project to proceed. The Trustees also record with appreciation the great helpfulness shown by Lesley Taylor of Saint Andrew Press in the production of this volume and their indebtedness to the Revd Finlay Stewart for allowing the use of photographs.

There are many ways in which the legacy of Henry Drummond is still with us today. It is the hope of the Trustees that the present volume will be one significant form of commemoration.

Ian Sinclair
on behalf of the Drummond Trustees
STIRLING 1996

The Life of
HENRY
DRUMMOND
(1851-1897)

by
George Adam Smith

A shortened version
of the book published
by Hodder & Stoughton
in 1899

CHAPTER 1

As We knew Him

THERE are hundreds of men and women who are sure that Henry Drummond's was the most Christian life they ever knew.

Perhaps the most conspicuous service which Henry Drummond rendered to his generation was to show them a Christianity which was perfectly natural. You met him somewhere, a tall, well-dressed gentleman, with a brightness on his face, who seemed to carry no cares and to know neither presumption nor timidity. You spoke, and found him keen for any of a hundred interests.

He was sure to find out what interested you, and listen by the hour. Sometimes you would remember that he was Drummond the evangelist, Drummond the author of books which measured their circulation by scores of thousands. Yet there was no assumption of superiority nor any ambition to gain influence. He was one of the purest, most unselfish, most reverent souls you ever knew, but you would not have called him a saint.

That he had 'a genius for friendship' goes without saying, for he was rich in the humility, the patience and the powers of trust which such a genius implies.

The longer you knew him, the fact which most impressed you was that he seldom talked about himself and never about that inner self which for praise or for sympathy is in many men so clamant.

He had learned the secret of St Paul – 'not to look upon his own things, but upon the affairs of others.' But Drummond had been taught another secret of the Apostle. St Paul everywhere links our life in Christ to the great cosmic processes. To Henry Drummond,

Christianity was the crown of the evolution of the whole universe. The drama which absorbed him is upon a stage infinitely wider than the moral life of man. The soul, in its battle against evil, in its service for Christ, is no accident nor exception, thrown upon a world all hostile to its feeble spirit. But the forces it represents are the primal forces of the Universe. I think it is in this belief, that, at least in part, we find the secret of the serenity, the healthy objectiveness and the courage of Henry Drummond's faith.

It was certainly on such grounds that in the prime of his teaching he sought to win the reason of men for religion. He had an ill-will – one might say a horror – at rousing the emotions before he had secured the conviction of the intellect. He always began by the presentation of facts, by the unfolding of laws, and trust in these and obedience to them was, in his teaching, religion. Yet he never thought of these laws as impersonal, for the greatest were love and the will that men should be holy, and he spoke of their power and their tenderness as they who sing, 'Underneath are the everlasting arms'. He had an open vision of love wrought into the very foundation of the world.

The source and the return of all his interest in men and of all his trust in God was Jesus Christ. There was no word of Christ more often upon his lips than this: 'Abide in me and I in you, for without me ye can do nothing.'

Mr Moody [the famous evangelist] has said: 'No words of mine can better describe his life or character than those in which he has presented to us "The Greatest Thing in the World".' As you read what he terms the analysis of love [in the thirteenth chapter of First Corinthians], you find that all its ingredients were interwoven into his daily life. It could be said of him truthfully, as it was said of the early apostles, 'that men took knowledge of him, that he had been with Jesus'.

Let us take the testimony of Sir Archibald Geikie. When he became the first Professor of Geology in Edinburgh, Drummond was his first student. They travelled [widely] together: 'I have never met with a man in whom transparent integrity, high moral purpose, sweetness of disposition, and exuberant helpfulness were more happily combined with wide culture, poetic imagination, and scientific sympathies than they were in Henry Drummond.'

His first religious ministry was neither of books nor of public speech. He blamed the lack of personal dealing as the great fault of the organised religion of his time, and he was drawn to work in the inquiry rooms of the Revival of 1873-85.

Very few men in our day can have touched the springs of so many lives. Like all his friends, I know that hundreds of men and women had gone to him, and by him had been inspired with new hope of their betterment and new faith in God. His influence was like nothing so much as the influence of one of the greater mediaeval saints – who yet worked in a smaller world than he, and with a language that travelled more slowly. Men and women sought him who were of every rank of life and of almost every nation under the sun. He was prophet and priest to hosts of individuals.

As to the growth, or change, of his opinions, certain lines of that growth follow some of the most interesting religious and intellectual developments of our time. Here was a young man, trained in an evangelical family and in the school of the older orthodoxy, who consecrated his youth to the service of Christ, and never all his life lost his faith in Christ as his Lord and Saviour, or in Christ's divinity or in the power of His Atonement; but who grew away from many of the doctrines which, when he was young, were still regarded by the Churches as equally well assured and indispensable to the creed of a Christian: such as, for instance, belief in the literal inspiration and equal divinity of all parts of the Bible.

Parallel to this change in his views of Scripture, and contributory to it, is the very interesting growth of the influence wrought upon his religious opinions by physical science and that discovery of natural laws in which his generation had been so active.

But besides these two developments there is a third, which is also characteristic of our time. To Drummond in his youth, religion was an affair of the individual. Yet he so greatly extended his sympathy and his experience, he so developed the civic conscience, as to become one of the principal exponents in our day of the social duties of religion. Thus his career is typical of the influence upon the older Christian orthodoxy of the three great intellectual movements of our time [*ie* the late nineteenth century] – historical criticism, physical science, and socialism (in the broad and unsectarian meaning of that much-abused word).

Again, Henry Drummond was a traveller, with keen powers of observation, a scientific training, and a great sympathy with human life on its lowest levels and outside edge.

Finally, Henry Drummond was a writer of books, which brought him no little fame in the world. As to the style in which they are written, the even and limpid pages of his books are the expression of his equable and transparent temper. And as his character was the outcome of a genuine discipline, so his style was the fruit of hard labour and an unsparing will.

But all these talents and experiences were only parts of a rare and radiant whole, of which any biography can with them all offer only an imperfect reflection.

CHAPTER 2

School and College

HENRY Drummond came of a family resident for some generations near the town of Stirling. His grandfather, William
Drummond, appears to have been a man who thought for himself
on matters of religion. He had eleven sons. Of these, Henry, who
was the father of our Henry, became head of the firm of William
Drummond and Sons, Seedsmen and Nurserymen at Stirling and
Dublin. One of his brothers was Peter, who withdrew from the
firm in order to give his energies to the Stirling Tract Enterprise,
of which he was the founder.

Mr Henry Drummond, senior, was a man of great worth, [who]
was in the front of every good cause in Stirling. He was a Justice of
the Peace, President of the YMCA, and an elder in the Free North
Church under the ministry of the Revd Dr Beith.

Mr and Mrs Drummond had four sons and two daughters.
Henry was born in Stirling on 17 August 1851. His father's house
was then No 1 Park Place, the house next to 'Glenelm', which
afterwards became the family home. The houses stand on the
southern side of the King's Park, and look across to the rock and
castle. The park was the children's playground.

Henry and James [his brother] were sent first to a ladies'
school, and, when Henry was six or seven, to the High School of
Stirling, where he remained till he was twelve.

At that time the High, or Grammar, Schools of Scotland were of
various quality, depending on the character of the headmaster. The
school discipline did not extend beyond the classes. Preparation

was done at home, and a boy's habits of study largely depended on his guardian.

A day schoolboy lives in no vacuum; at home, in the streets, and in the country around, there are a hundred healthy interests of which boarding schools know little. In Henry's time boys had their rounders, a primitive football, 'Scots and English', 'Thieves and Police', and other running games, sham fights and sieges – all hard and healthy sports. It was a breezy, healthy life, and not the least part of its health was the way the 'town's school' brought all classes of the 'town's bairns' into rivalry, both of work and play.

The boys were made to write essays. They found their way to the Macfarlane Free Library, and in that dingy place hunted up their subjects in the few encyclopaedias. Their own reading was mainly in Ballantyne's stories or Beadle's 'American Library' of sixpenny books.

In school the English class was always opened with prayer. Every Monday morning a verse of a Psalm was repeated and a chapter read, and every Friday morning a question was asked from the Catechism.

Mr Drummond did not send his children to a Sabbath school, but on Sunday they gathered to sing hymns, and were catechised and formally addressed by their father. They went twice to church.

The Revd John H McCulloch writes: 'Henry was more prominent in the playground than in the class. I think of him most of all in the English department. Henry more than once obtained the reading prize. I think the skill which was then developed largely helped to make him the speaker he subsequently became.'

He was a rapid learner, but volatile, careless of hours, and often late for meals. He took to cricket with enthusiasm and some skill; both at Stirling and at Crieff he kept wickets for the eleven. But fishing was his favourite sport – his first rod a bamboo cane with a string at the end of it. Around [his fishing] excursions lay one of the most glorious landscapes even in Scotland. He has not written of what all this was to him. But after he had seen most of the world, whenever he came back to Stirling, he would take his old walk round the Castle, and say to his brother, 'Man, there's no place like this – no place like Scotland'.

When Henry was twelve, James and he were sent to Morrison's Academy at Crieff. After two years James entered his father's business, but Henry stayed on to prepare for the University. A series of letters to James and his parents record the details of a very happy life. Throughout there beats a strong sympathy with all at home. The habit thus formed was retained. Till the end Drummond almost never missed writing his mother so that she should get a letter every Saturday night.

This natural boyhood, eagerly enjoyed, was the secret of his life-long sympathy with boys.

If the area of religious experience was denominational, this involved no bitterness, but merely an ignorance of the works of other churches, which, Henry once naively told me, was the source to him afterwards of the most delightful surprises at the great amount of good in the world.

His schoolmates have emphasised the unselfishness of the boy, and unselfishness was the note of his life to the end. But the most beautiful thing which the letters reveal is the full confidence between parents and children.

In July 1866 Henry left Crieff with prizes for Latin and English and for an essay on 'War and Peace'. In October, being 15 years of age and very small, he matriculated at Edinburgh University.

In the first year of Arts in those days, the students were either boys or bearded men fresh from the plough and the workshop. They worked through several Latin and Greek authors, not the most difficult, did a heap of prose exercises, and learned several books of *Euclid* with a little algebra. The freshmen formed a debating society, the 'Philomathic'. Besides the usual historical questions to which schoolboys devote themselves, it determined week by week the rank of the great stars of literature, and solved the most abstruse economic problems; but it was also practical, reviewing once a year the policy of the Government. In Drummond's time it disposed of the Irish Church, decided against the education of women, reformed the Game Laws, and drew up a new programme of the Arts curriculum.

Partly through a dislike of Classics, Henry took an erratic course through Arts. It was under Professor Tait [with whom he took Mathematics and Natural Philosophy] that Drummond first woke up to something more than the performance of routine, and his notebooks have full transcripts of the lectures with diagrams of the experiments.

In the spring of 1869 he passed the examination in Mathematics and Physics for the Degree of Master of Arts. In April 1870 he closed his Arts course by passing the degree examinations in Mental Philosophy. 'I had never courage,' he wrote, 'to attempt the Classical department of the MA.'

During his divinity course he came back to the University for Botany, Chemistry, Zoology, in which he took the second place, and Geology, in which he won the class medal. But although he tried twice, he failed to pass the first part of the Bachelor of Science examination, and left the University without a degree.

Drummond also contributed to the debates in the 'Philomathic', speaking against the Irish Church and in favour of the education of women, the latter on the grounds of the 'awful crime of leaving any mind untrained, and of the terribly unintellectual state of the average girl of the period'!

He had begun to form a library, and to read for himself. He had fallen under the spell of John Ruskin.

At the election of Lord Rector of the University in 1868, he canvassed for him, as against the political candidates.

In 1870 he delivered his valedictory address as President of the 'Philomathic', and after expounding the advantages of debate, contrasted the lecture, conversation, and reading, as means of gaining knowledge. 'The lecture,' he says, 'is the best means. If it has fallen into disrepute in our day, that is because there are no good lecturers.' He passes on to reading: 'Most neglect the great end of reading. The thing sought is not what you will get in an author, but what the author will enable you to find in yourself' ....

'The great danger of reading is superficiality. Many read far too much.'

Notes in preparation for an article in the *Stirling Observer* – Drummond's earliest published writing – reveal a keen sense of beauty and an extraordinary care in sketching natural facts. [They show] how diligently and how sanely he prepared the clear and brilliant style for which he afterwards became famous.

There is no evidence in any of his essays at this time of an original capacity of thought; but there is abundant proof of unusually keen powers of observation, of a fine and healthy taste in letters, and of distinct powers of illustration and interpretation.

'One thing,' writes Mr McCulloch, 'which struck me at college was the fashion in which Drummond laid himself out, in a quiet way, thoroughly to know how those around him looked at things. Everybody liked him too, because he was never inquisitorial.'

During his university course, Drummond had shot up into a tall man, moving with a litheness and a spring that were all his own. A fellow student thus remembers him: 'He seemed to have no companions as the other students had, but was only one of them, handsome, bright and silent. He struck me as one possessed by great thoughts which were polarising in his mind and giving a happy expression to his face.'

CHAPTER 3

Preparation for the Ministry

WHILE Henry Drummond was a student, he attended some mission services at Cambusbarron [near Stirling]; he was profoundly impressed by the addresses he heard, and soon after told his father that he wished to enter the ministry.

The first notice of his intentions occurs in a letter to a fellow student of date April 1870:'Are you not sorry to leave the University? I feel it very much. Altho' I intend to enter the Church Hall next winter, it is still a degeneracy to go from an ancient University to a nameless college. Happily I shall still be a student.'

In the summer a religious crisis happened to Drummond in the form we should have expected from his upbringing. 'The only misery I have endured has been of my own creation – the consciousness of my own guilt before God.' When, as in his case, sincerity was the atmosphere of the home in which [the Evangelical movement's] doctrines were taught, it succeeded in creating in the children a tender and scrupulous conscience; and by urging them above all to the consideration of their personal relation to a just and merciful God, it strongly developed the sense of their individual responsibility. Pure minds like Henry Drummond's will feel powerfully the accumulated memories of a lifetime of God's common mercies, and of His daily patience with their wilful ways. Once, when talking of 'sudden conversions', I asked Drummond whether he had passed through one. 'No,' he said. 'But I have seen too many ever to doubt their reality.'

In November 1870 Drummond entered New College, Edinburgh, the youngest of 25 or thirty students who formed the First Year. At New College there are always some hundred regular students of the Church, besides twenty or thirty others from America, Ireland, and the Reformed Churches of the Continent of Europe. Among a hundred men studying for the same profession, there is bound to be a closer fellowship than among the far larger number of students and the more scattered interests of the Arts course. Given a certain proportion of able men, the atmosphere of the College was always genial and stimulating.

The First Year's classes were Junior Hebrew, Apologetics, Natural Science, and lectures on Evangelistic Theology from the famous missionary to India, Dr Duff. There were not many of the Edinburgh students who gave themselves to foreign missions. We sorely tried the great missionary's heart. Drummond shared the common apathy. He needed the touch with the concrete; and this he got years afterwards on his travels in Africa and the East, with the result that among all testimonies to foreign missions in the last half-century, none are more thorough or more sincere than his.

It was to Natural Science that Drummond chiefly devoted himself at New College, and he easily carried off the first prize. But he worked hard both at Hebrew and Apologetics. Besides the grammar, Dr Davidson then gave to the First Year a few lectures introductory to the Higher Criticism of the Pentateuch. That was sufficient to break up the mechanical ideas of inspiration which then prevailed in the Churches, while, with the teacher's own wonderful insight into the spiritual meaning of Scripture, it made the student's own use of his Bible more rational and lively, and laid upon a sounder basis the proof of a real revelation in the Old Testament.

A year later Drummond wrote for the class of Systematic Theology an essay on 'The Doctrine of Creation'. He put the question whether the world, as explained by Modern Science, was irreconcilable with the Scriptural statement of Creation. Granted that Natural Selection and Evolution are facts, [he argued,] they are not irreconcilable with the belief that God has created and sustains the world. On the contrary, 'this belief can allow them a very prominent place', but on the distinct understanding that this place has been previously assigned them by God, and that they are under his supervision and care. Looked at from this point of view, the principle of Natural Selection becomes a real and beautiful acquisition to Natural Theology.

The same year Drummond delivered an address on Evolution. He affirmed the principle of Development as an eternal principle, but he criticised Darwin's enunciation of it on three points: 'He ignores the existence of a personal God, denies God's sovereignty, and denies the existence of design in the Universe.'

These notes of college essays, juvenile and crude, are of interest as the first steps of Drummond's mind towards the work of his later years. But at this stage Drummond did not see how to apply the principle of Development to the origins of Scripture and the story of Revelation.

At the very point at which a theological student is most disposed to be sceptical – the close of his first session in theology – Drummond accepted Orthodox Christianity, not after any passionate struggle towards the contrary, not with any strength of original thought, but upon a full knowledge of the issues and after serious consideration. The absence of revolt is characteristic. To Drummond the Christian experience of faith was one not so much of struggle as of growth.

The sessions at New College – 1871-72 and 1872-73 – were occupied with the regular classes: Senior Hebrew, New Testament Exegesis, Systematic Theology, and Church History. His reading included Ruskin, George Eliot, Thomas Carlyle, and much poetry.

At the close of his third session, in April 1873, Drummond went to a German University for the summer semester. Drummond chose Tübingen. I do not know what classes he attended. More important was the general life and atmosphere of the place, and this he enjoyed to the full.

Who does not, that goes to Tübingen straight from a Scottish winter? The glory of the southern spring and summer, the first sight of vineyards, and the first tramp through a real forest, the mediaeval castles and churches, the hospitality and '*gemütlichkeit*' of the Swabians, the genuine piety, with other forms and larger liberties than Scottish religion has allowed itself, the first impressions of the thoroughness of German scholarship, the gradual mastery of the great language and the entrance upon the vast new literature – with all these it is not wonderful that so many of us at Tübingen should have wakened for the first time to what Nature is, and even found there in a sense the second birth of our intellect.

Drummond made a great impression on the Tübingen people, as he did everywhere by his sunniness and his sympathy.

On his return from Germany, Drummond resolved to postpone his fourth session at New College for a year or two, in order to give himself to the study of Natural Science and to regular Mission work. He retained, however, his position as President of the Theological Society. Dr Stalker sends me the following recollection: 'He electrified us with an essay on Spiritual Diagnosis. He contrasted the clinical work of a medical student with the total absence of any direct dealing with men in a theological curriculum, and maintained that a minister can do far more good by "buttonholing" individuals than by preaching sermons. Within a month Mr Moody had arrived, and in his meetings Henry was putting his speculations into practice.'

The same week he started operations as missionary in the Riego Street Mission at St Cuthbert's Free Church, Edinburgh. He records, 'The first time I ever faced an audience, sensations not remarkable. When my turn came, I trembled on standing up – considerably all through. Tremor in voice. I should think not perceived, mind kept perfectly clear and cool. Voice seemed not my own, but a new voice. Prayer was simple and to the point. I was more than satisfied with the result. Of course there was nothing of my doing in it.'

He wrote out his prayers very carefully, and prepared full notes for his addresses. 'Address – what shall I say? I think it must have been very poor, particularly as to the delivery. Was not the least nervous, but did not know exactly where to look.'

The following week a religious movement began in Edinburgh and spread over the country, which caught up the stammering evangelist to a higher platform, and gave him his first extra-ordinary influence and fame among men.

CHAPTER 4

The Great Mission 1873-1875

TOWARDS the end of the summer of 1873, two Americans landed at Liverpool, with the purpose of holding religious meetings in the large cities of England. Their names were Dwight L Moody, the preacher, and Ira D Sankey, the singer.

The Revd John Kelman of Leith, by what he witnessed at Sunderland and at Newcastle, was convinced of the real power of the movement and gave the evangelists an invitation to Scotland.

In Edinburgh, after inauspicious beginnings, every week the tide rose. Members of all the Protestant denominations professed themselves quickened. The prejudices of those who for years had resisted every attempt to introduce instrumental music into public worship were overcome. The most respected leaders of religion spoke from the evangelists' platforms, helped in the inquiry rooms and instructed the young converts.

The secret of all this lay open. The evangelists themselves were obviously men of sincerity and power. They were practical, they were sane. Mr Moody suffered no fools, and every symptom of the hysteria which often breaks out in such movements was promptly suppressed.

The preaching won Scotsmen's hearts by its loyalty to the Bible and its expository character. Mr Moody's gospel was the gospel of an Incarnate Saviour – to cleanse the cities of their foulness, organise the helpless and neglected, succour the fallen and gather the friendless into families. We have forgotten how often Mr Moody enforced the civic duties of our faith. He reawakened in Scotland not a few echoes of [Thomas] Chalmers. Hardly educated himself, he emphasised the education of the ministry. But the chief features of the movement were its prayerfulness and its ethical temper. The theology was stiff, but it was never abstract. The words of the hymns were poor, and the music little better, but mystical power came with them.

The movement spread over Scotland. Messrs Moody and Sankey spent the spring of 1874 in Glasgow and other towns in the west. Everything happened that had happened in Edinburgh, but on a larger scale. The custom was to reserve every Monday evening for a meeting of converts. At the last one in Glasgow there were 3500 present.

Nor did the work diminish in a district when the evangelists passed on. In Edinburgh it was said that the results rather increased after their farewell meeting. One thousand two hundred converts were visited every fortnight for the next two years. This careful supervision had the best effect on the churches, in which the number of young communicants was largely increased. Ministers themselves were quickened.

But the power spread beyond the congregations, and one of the most striking features of the movement was the social and philanthropic work which it stimulated. Mr Moody inspired the Christians of Glasgow to attempt missions to the criminal classes and the relief of the friendless. New impulses were given to the Orphan Homes of Scotland, founded in 1871 by Mr Quarrier. Mr Moody gave great attention to Young Men's Christian Associations. 'Do not, however,' he said, 'put the Association in place of the Church; it is a handmaid of the Church.' We may express the wish that the manly and liberal views of the evangelist had been carried out by *all* the institutions which he did so much to invigorate.

[As for] Henry Drummond, with the date of the evangelists' arrival in Edinburgh, the diary of his own work [at the Riego Street Mission] stops short, as if he had been suddenly carried off upon some larger stream.

We can understand how his keen mind watched the movement.

His accent, his style, his tastes were at the other pole from those of the evangelists. His speech was quiet and restrained, he had a perilous sense of humour, and I do not think that he ever really cared for large public meetings. Nor did the social possibilities of the movement attract him; at this time he had not the civic conscience. But from the first he felt Mr Moody's sincerity, and the practical wisdom of the new methods. The inquiry meetings bridged the gap between preacher and hearer, and brought them together before God. On his side, Mr Moody was feeling the need of a young man to take charge of the meetings for young men, and it is a tribute to his insight that he chose one whose style and tastes were so different from his own.

At first Drummond was employed, like other students, only in the inquiry room.

> As the marvellous work developed in Edinburgh, the news of course flew in every direction, and requests came pouring in from all parts of the country for speakers to come and describe it. The descriptions were combined with evangelistic addresses. This went on for months, and Drummond was in the thick of it all the time.
>
> ~ *Revd James Stalker* ~

Others remember that Mr Moody himself was in Elgin, and, to Drummond's surprise, opened the door to him when he arrived there. It was, in fact, because of what he heard, or saw, of the work in Elgin that Mr Moody sent Drummond to Sunderland – the first instance of his policy of setting Drummond to continue the work among young men at places which Mr Sankey and he had visited.

The work at Sunderland began, as elsewhere, among the middle classes and spread to the working men. Members of the Society of Friends were among the hardest workers, but all the Nonconformist ministers gave their help. But there appears to have been no excitement, and the large daily gatherings for prayer were conducted with deep earnestness. Parents were so stirred that arrangements were made to extend the public services to children, and in this delicate work – the propriety of which Drummond afterwards questioned, believing that religion comes to a child most naturally through its home – some amount of real good was done, in spite of the artificial and premature 'experiences' that such a movement always forces.

From Drummond's letters to his parents:

SUNDERLAND:
Generally there are about 100 inquirers in all every night, and as most of these come to the light before leaving, you may imagine the wonderful nature of the work going on around us.

HARTLEPOOL:
The general impression in Sunderland is that the work is just beginning, and although we have left the place, I expect we shall have to go back again.

HEXHAM:
If the work had been bad, I should have been with you tomorrow, but I see now it will not do to break off. You know, every night counts. As to my health, I think I am stronger than ever.

Meetings of 3000 and 4000, daily addresses to young men, a constant confessional, crowds of anxious inquirers, invitations from all quarters, the success of the work obviously dependent upon his presence – conceive of all this falling to a man not quite 23! Yet there is abundant evidence in his letters that he did not lose his head. He remained shrewd and sensible, and it was already noticed of him that, as in all his later years, he never betrayed either on or off the platform one secret of the many hundreds that must have been confided to him by those who sought his counsel and inspiration. The Sunderland Mission made Drummond a man. He won from it not only the power of organising and leading his fellow men, but that insight into character, that knowledge of life on its lowest as on its highest levels, that power of interest in every individual he met, which so brilliantly distinguished him, and in later years made us who were his friends feel as if his experience and his sympathy were exhaustless.

When Messrs Moody and Sankey moved to Londonderry, they sent for Drummond.

LONDONDERRY:

I think Derry beats any work I have been in by a great deal. I think it was one of the most impressive meetings I have seen …. I suppose I am fairly engaged now to follow Moody all winter and take his young men's meetings. I cannot help thinking more and more every day that this is the work God has planned for me this session. Why I should have such a tremendous privilege is the only mystery to me.

To Dublin the evangelists went with some trepidation, but the work ultimately reached even greater dimensions than the evangelists had yet experienced. The increase was partly due to the hearty co-operation, for the first time in the history of the movement, of the Episcopalian clergy, while the daily press chronicled the meetings with a fullness never displayed elsewhere.

Many Roman Catholics frequented the meetings. There was unity among Christians. An 'all-day' meeting was attended by 15,000 people, [including] nearly 1000 ministers.

Moody himself spoke on Sectarianism:

If you have a minister that preaches Christ, stand by him. You will get nothing but trouble and pride by leaving him. There are people who consider that denouncing churches and finding fault with ministers is 'bearing testimony'. These people will 'bear testimony' for years, and that is all Christ gets from them. I warn you, beware of trying to get people away from the folds where they have been fed. The moment we begin to lift up our little party or our Church, then the Spirit of God seems to leave, and there is no more conversion.

Drummond himself said that in Dublin hundreds had sent in their names as converts: mainly artisans, shopmen and clerks. Some of them were quite uneducated; the first result of their conversion to Christ was usually a strong passion to learn to read.

In Sheffield, in Birmingham, and in Liverpool, the same features marked the work: enormous meetings from the very start, at first small, ultimately large numbers of converts; the quickening of church life, a very widespread interest among the general population, the historic halls of the cities crammed on Sunday evenings, and, in spite of overflow meetings, the streets around filled in the rain and the darkness with crowds singing hymns.

SHEFFIELD:

I was real sorry to leave my little Manchester meeting which hard labour had worked up after much discouragement. Of course, it is a much smaller thing than the work here. On Wednesday night I suppose my audience would count about 300, while last night in Sheffield it was about as many thousands. I think the work here is going to be splendid. All classes are moved, from the Mayor to the beggar.

BIRMINGHAM:

Moody is not at all the worse for this great work here, speaking to 15,000 people every night. These figures are not exaggerated. He is very careful, and he says so himself.

LIVERPOOL:

I got a treat last night. Moody sat up alone with me till near one o'clock telling the story of his life. A reporter might have made his fortune out of it!

The mission of Messrs Moody and Sankey to Liverpool produced greater results than they had achieved in any other town.

A witness says of one meeting: 'No startling appeals had been listened to: there was nothing to excite anyone, yet the close-pressed phalanx of city merchants and ministers on the platform had a struggle to repress emotion.'

Drummond's meetings with young men had 1000 or 1200 every night.

LIVERPOOL:
The people here are very kind: I have got to know nearly the whole religious public, and could be out to breakfast, dinner or tea every day; but I decline all invitations.

LIVERPOOL:
I have a theatre full of young men to 'farewell address' at 3, a circus full of working men at 4, another theatre full of men and women at 7 in Birkenhead, and the usual circus full of young men at 9.

The London mission was begun on 14 March in the Agricultural Hall, Islington, which was seated for 13,000 persons, with standing room for a thousand or two more. The evening meeting for men filled it to its utmost capacity, and during the following week the gatherings varied from 4000 to 14,000. With scarcely an exception, the daily press 'spoke of the work in terms of respect, even of hopefulness' (Dr R W Dale), and the interest in it spread to all classes of society.

Drummond came to London about the close of the first week in April.

LONDON:
London has been a fair success only, I mean after Liverpool. Many things were against work among the young men. After this week I go 'away down east', as Moody would say. There we have pitched a tent to hold a thousand young men, which we expect to have crammed every night. After setting that agoing, I think the next move will be to the Haymarket Opera House .... I have been writing Moody's sermons all day: you know they are being published under my most distinguished editorship.

How would you like to see an acre of people? That is exactly the size of the audience to which Mr Moody preaches every night in the East of London.

Your huge remittance came to me all right this morning with James. I shall ride once more upon a bus.

(Drummond appears to have refused, during this mission, all remuneration, and only sometimes to have taken all his expenses.)

The greatest event in my programme this week was a large children's meeting in the Opera House. I am to have another on Saturday along with Mr Sankey, and expect a great hubbub!

Twenty five years have passed [ie, by 1898] since the American evangelists began their mission to Great Britain. No one can doubt the enormous power of the movement so long as it lasted. What has it left behind?

Probably there never was a movement of the kind in which religious extravagance and dissipation were more honestly discouraged. The preaching was Biblical and ethical. The doctrines were those of Catholic Christianity. The salvation proclaimed was, with some exceptions, salvation not from hell, but from sin.

To form, however, a just appreciation of the movement, we must recall some things upon the other side. There was a proportion of the comfortable middle class, who spent their leisure in running from meeting to meeting, and who from that day to this act as if they believed that such conventions were at once the highest duty and happiest privilege of religion. Their excitement and the habits which it has formed have not been beneficial to Christianity.

There was a temptation to ignore all religious experience which lay outside the definite theology of the movement, and a stubborn refusal to recognise the manifest fruits of God's spirit apart from the formulas and processes by which its converts had arrived at the truth. Another form of this vice was the unwillingness to see in Scripture any facts save such as might be used to confirm a very narrow theory of inspiration. During the last 25 years, much of Evangelicalism has been beset by narrowness, inaccuracy and the fear to acknowledge some of the healthiest and divinest movements of our time.

But how much falls to the bright side of the reckoning! This Mission lifted tens of thousands of persons already trained in religion to a more clear and decided consciousness of their Christianity. It baptised crowds in the Spirit of Jesus, and opened the eyes of innumerable men and women to the reality of the great facts of repentance and conversion. The Spirit of our God works among us in many other ways than by 'revivals' and church services, and the evangelical movement has required every iota of the influence of science to teach it tolerance, accuracy and fearlessness of facts, and all the strength of the Socialist movement to reawaken within it that sense of civic and economic duty, by which the older evangelicalism of Wilberforce, Chalmers and Shaftesbury was so nobly distinguished. Among the men who have seen this have been many – very many – converts of the two American evangelists, whom God in His grace sent to our shores.

We shall see in the rest of this biography how Drummond contributed to this wider evangelicalism of our day: meantime let us understand how he helped the movement, and how the movement helped him.

★   ★   ★

From April 1874 to July 1875 Drummond followed up the work of the evangelists in the cities of Ireland and England, and he laboured by their side in London. During this period he probably composed the first drafts of most of the discourses for which in later years he became famous, [such as] his great address on 'Seek ye first the Kingdom of God'. He had also spoken on 'The Greatest Thing in the World' and 'The Changed Life'.

He stuck close to the Bible. He used the incidents of the Old Testament to enforce the teaching of the New, just as older evangelists did. But his manner of presentation was entirely his own, and in speaking to young men he never forget that he must put things differently from the way in which things were put to their elders.

He acted on the principle that 'a young man's religion could not be the same as his grandmother's'. His style of speaking was simple and clear; he kept to the concrete, and already revealed his famous powers of illustration and analogy. His manner was quiet and self-possessed. He had not a strong, nor in any way a remarkable voice, but he used it easily in the largest meetings.

Who could ever again fear or fail that at 23 had organised the meetings he had to organise, or had faced the crowds he had to face night after night! But his opportunities would have been nothing without himself. Not experience only, nor coolness, but quick sympathy which does not always go with coolness, rapid appreciation of other men's gifts, and the power of enlisting them, perfect courtesy, good humour, and a strong dramatic interest, made him an ideal chairman. Indeed, it is his biographer's despair to explain to those who never felt it the equal charm and force which came out from him.

Dr Stalker has written:

At that time we had many experiences which have ever since made Christ intelligible, and the Book of the Acts of the Apostles especially has a meaning to those who have passed through such a movement which it could scarcely, I think, have for any one else.

To associate Henry Drummond only with meetings and addresses would be to misrepresent him. He took great trouble with every person in the inquiry rooms, as much trouble and interest as if each was a large meeting. His sympathy won their confidence, and men felt he was not a voice merely, but a friend. He sent a man away feeling that he was trusted once more, not only by his friend, but by Christ, by God.

His patience with odd characters was his friends' wonder to the end. One good lady wrote that she is 'sure he is her friend, wants to introduce him to her eleven children and 19 grandchildren, and has asked them all to a one o'clock dinner tomorrow to meet him'.

Men and women of the idle middle classes sent him verses and tracts to publish. There were countless appeals for employment, requests for sermons, for collections from clergymen whose churches were in debt.

One of the kinds of appeal that gave him most trouble was that from well-intentioned people who wanted him to speak to their young relatives about their souls, when these young relatives had no wish to be spoken to. On the occasions when he could not escape such conversations, he would begin thus: 'I suppose you know this is a put-up job'; or thus: 'What you are suffering from is too much religion, isn't it?' His insight was marvellous.

Thus at 23 he saw life on all its sides, learned the secrets of countless characters, and was trusted by thousands of his fellow men.

Yet he stepped from it all unspoiled, and the next session went quietly back to college.

CHAPTER 5

Back to College

HENRY Drummond did not go back to college without a struggle. Invitations to conduct missions poured in upon him from all quarters. But his parents had renewed their pressure upon him, and his wisest friends warned him of the perils of the wandering evangelist's life.

He was still hesitating when he went in August 1875 to spend a holiday with his friend Robert W Barbour at Bonskeid, Perthshire. Barbour had just finished a brilliant course at Edinburgh University, but had found time with it all for work among young men in Moody and Sankey's mission. Drummond and he discussed their future at some length, and Barbour's mother, although fully aware of Drummond's power as an evangelist, lent her influence to persuade him to complete his studies for the regular ministry. Drummond later described [her argument] thus: 'Perhaps a few years of enthusiasm and blessing, then carelessness: no study, no spiritual fruits, too often a sad collapse.' That, he said, sent him back to his last year at college.

How strong the temptations were to continue as an evangelist may be felt from a letter from Mr Moody: 'I miss you more than I can tell. You do not know how much I want you with me. Come if you possibly can.'

When Drummond came back to college, the men who shared with him the first and most profound experiences of the great Mission were already in the ministry, and while the students regarded himself with respect and admiration, their religious interests were far from being identified with the methods of the Mission.

The First Year contained five men with first class honours, and there was a strong intellectual rivalry. The debates in the Theological Society were vigorous, the chief interest being in Dogmatic Theology. The students were helped by the lectures of Dr Davidson, who taught them Old Testament Theology, not as the dogmas of a Church, but as the living experience of a great people. We also found of value Muller's 'Doctrine of Sin'. The effect upon the debates was that the best men argued for truths which they had lived upon or had seen working in the lives of others; it can be imagined how much they were helped in this by their experience of the Great Revival, in which many of them had taken part. The practical and the theoretical thus developed in close co-operation.

Into this life Drummond slipped from his great experience very quietly. The younger men, who had not been in the Moody movement, were a little afraid of him and of the chance of his tackling us upon our own religious life. But we [ie George Adam Smith and other students] found him unaggressive, treating us as equals, willing to be our friend, entering into our fun. Soon our feeling of his friendliness deepened to gratitude for his power of doing us good. We felt that he was interested in us, and his interest, being without officiousness, won our confidence. 'He and Robert Barbour,' said a fellow student, 'were the only two men I ever knew who helped you to feel that you were stronger and your work better than you had dared to believe.'

On his part, Drummond laid himself out to learn from the new men among whom he was thrown. The effort of the leaders of the college to find a dogmatic based on experience enlisted his sympathy, and this year he mastered Muller's great work on Sin, which had ever afterwards some influence on his thinking.

The facts of Old Testament criticism made a deep impression on his mind. He did not yet throw off the narrow theory of inspiration, but all he learned engaged his sympathies for the great movement which was now rising in Scotland under the hands of Professor William Robertson Smith.

Drummond did not forget the duties of an evangelist. He

engaged the 'Gaiety' Music Hall for a number of Sunday evenings, for meetings of men. When he spoke, the hall was full.

From these meetings came the name of the Gaiety Club, which met every spring from a Monday to a Saturday at some country inn, and for 22 years these annual gatherings have been sustained without a break. Drummond attended every one of them, save three. This was the innermost circle among his countless friends.

In April 1876 Drummond finished his four years' course of Divinity and passed the second part of the exit examination. He received several invitations from ministers to become their assistant, and several others to preach as a candidate for vacant charges, but he declined them all, and though, in the ordinary course, he should have taken licence to preach, he was still so uncertain of his future that he postponed this first step towards the full orders of the Presbyterian ministry.

In September he was preaching and evangelising in various parts of Scotland. In the end of the year he accepted an invitation from Mr Wilson of the Barclay Church [in Edinburgh] to assist him for some months.

EDINBURGH:

I am in full swing of work and very happy. Rather I should say, I am very interested. I do not feel that I am in my life-work, however, but am certain it is a splendid and unique training for it, and I am sure I shall thank God for it long afterwards. The unengaged nights are generally occupied with meetings of some sort, or private work with inquirers. Indeed, this last is the best part of it all.

The congregational routine was not to his taste, and he felt cramped.

In July he went for a tour in Norway with Robert Barbour, to whom he afterwards wrote:

Norway did me a world of good; it was a clear month out of reading, out of thinking, out of planning for the future, out of responsibility for others. I think this is the true holiday – to be one's simplest self, forget the past, and ignore the future. I never came back to work, to books, to Christianity, I might almost say, with such a spring; the world seemed new-born.

But Drummond, still uncertain of his future, was not happy. He went to New College to see what subjects were required for examination for licence, though he did not want to be licensed. He had been blamed (he says) as if he had given up the ministry, but he had never been a minister, nor wanted to be.

At college he found some numbers of *Nature* that had been accumulating for him, and then all his scientific studies came back upon him. In a day or two he noticed the death of Mr Keddie, the lecturer on Natural Science, in the Free College, Glasgow, and wrote to Principal Douglas to ask if it was any use his applying for the lectureship. On 17 September the General Assembly's College Committee appointed him to the lectureship for one session, and so he found the work that ultimately formed the profession and settled post after which he had been groping for two years.

During these years, Drummond had been much sustained by studying the teaching of the Bible upon the Will of God. He put the result in three sermons which he preached from the Barclay pulpit, and which now form the last of his volume *The Ideal Life*. But he summarised this in eight maxims, which he inscribed upon the fly-leaf of his Bible:

To find out God's Will

1. Pray.
2. Think.
3. Talk to wise people, but do not regard their decision as final.
4. Beware of the bias of your own will, but do not be too much afraid of it. (God never unnecessarily thwarts a man's nature and likings, and it is a mistake to think that His will is in the line of the disagreeable).

5. Meantime do the next thing (for doing God's will in small things is the best preparation for knowing it in great things).
6. When decision and action are necessary, go ahead.
7. Never reconsider the decision when it is finally acted upon, and
8. You will probably not find out till afterwards, perhaps long afterwards, that you have been led at all.

CHAPTER 6

Science and Religion

AT that time the Free Church felt herself obliged to supply for her students not only a theological curriculum, but a full Arts one as well. At New College, Edinburgh, in addition, a chair of Natural Science was founded. Other members of the Church, too, felt that science would so largely enter into Christian apologetics as to justify a separate class for its treatment, and a lectureship was established in the second Free Church College at Glasgow.

The students in Glasgow College varied from seventy to one hundred. Drummond lectured to the First Year. He chose to instruct the students in the rudiments of geology and botany and in the general methods of modern science. The salary was £150 a year, the lectures four a week, from the beginning of November to the end of March. Their preparation occupied the whole of his time [1877-8].

But the summer was free; and, eager for some religious work, he accepted an invitation to take charge of the Free Church of Scotland's station at Malta, in the absence of the chaplain.

'Malta,' he wrote to Robert Barbour, 'seems a most interesting place, thoroughly civilised by every nation on earth.'

In September, Drummond settled down again in Glasgow. He was happy in his lectureship, and very happy in his colleagues, with whom he was to work for 19 years on terms of the closest affection and confidence.

He had attached himself to Renfield Free Church under the ministry of Dr Marcus Dods, and was ordained as an elder. The congregation had recently adopted a mission station in Possilpark, and Dr Dods had offered the charge of it to Drummond, who entered upon his duties when he returned from Malta. In 1878 the population of Possilpark was said to be about 6000. They were nearly all well-to-do people, but in the autumn of 1878 the City of Glasgow Bank failed and cast hundreds of them out of work. It was a terrible winter, the social distress was aggravated and the ordinary labours of charity increased ten-fold. Owing to the number of honest families thrown into a distress to which they were absolutely new, the work required extraordinary patience and tact. But the rewards were great.

On Sabbath I preach twice, attend schools and classes. On Mondays I look after a bank, on Tuesdays I give a popular lecture. On Wednesdays a mothers' meeting in the afternoon, a lecture to children at seven, the congregational prayer-meeting at eight. The other two nights I visit the poor and the sick, or hold meetings elsewhere.

Although I have a church, I am not a minister yet. I have taken what we call 'licence' and which is often mistaken for ordination, but it is little more than a college certificate of a theological education, and my church is a mere appendage to my college work. By and by I give it up, and plunge into evangelism. I shall retain my college work – it will be corrective without being absorbing. I have had several calls this winter to be *ordained* to churches, but have refused them all. No one, however, can understand me.

I am to be away three months – all the time in the Far West. I am going with Professor Geikie. We are to geologise in the Rocky Mountains .... My College appointment was made permanent by my election to the Chair [*ie* lectureship] last Assembly [1879], so that there is no fear of my being a settled minister. I shall lecture five months and be a vagrant, or a city missionary, during the other seven. It is an odd life, but it suits me.

~ From letters to Mr and Mrs Stuart ~

The account of Drummond's geological expedition to the Rocky Mountains may be postponed. On his return, he found himself at Boston and in a curious dilemma. He had an invitation to meet Henry Wadsworth Longfellow and Oliver Wendell Holmes at dinner. But ...

> for me at least a visit to America would be much more than incomplete without a visit to Mr Moody and Mr Sankey .... Neither seemed the least changed, Mr Sankey down to the faultless set of his black necktie, Mr Moody to the chronic crush of his collar .... I had expected to find revival work in America more exciting, but although a deep work was beginning, everything was calm. There was movement but no agitation, there was power in the meetings but no frenzy. And the secret of that probably lay here, that in the speaker himself there was earnestness but no bigotry, and enthusiasm but no superstition.

~ *From a letter to* The Christian ~

No more signal proof could we have, both of Drummond's enthusiasm for the Gospel and of his loyalty to old friends.

Drummond returned to his third winter as lecturer on Natural Science, and as missionary in Possilpark. The years 1880 and 1881 passed away in this double work, without incident and almost without the break of a single holiday.

The case of Professor Robertson Smith [on a charge of contravening by his articles in the *Encyclopaedia Britannica* the doctrine of inspiration in the Westminster Confession of Faith] was proceeding from one church court to another. The truth is, it was not so much the trial of one man as the education of the whole church in face of the facts which Biblical criticism had recently presented to her. The Great Mission of 1873-75 had quickened the practical use of the Bible. But now came the necessary complement to all that, in the critical study of the Scriptures. Those who, with Professor Robertson Smith, instigated the latter, believed that Christ's promise of the Holy Spirit for the education of His Church was being fulfilled not less in the critical than in the experimental use of the

Bible; they defended criticism on the highest grounds of faith in God and loyalty to Christ.

At first Drummond could not but share the general uncertainty. He was not equipped with the knowledge of the original languages of the Bible which could have enabled him to form conclusions of his own. But his scientific training had given him a sense for facts, an appreciation of evidence. The Assembly of 1880 decided in Professor Smith's favour, and Drummond rejoiced at the decision. When it became apparent next spring that the General Assembly would remove Professor Smith from his chair, Drummond wrote in great sorrow, 'We are all much dejected here by the suicidal policy of the majority. It will be a very serious blow to the Church'.

Professor Robertson Smith was sacrificed, but whatever may have been the motives of the leaders of the majority, the Church was allowed to find room for methods of research and for views of inspiration more free from the errors of tradition and more true to the facts of Scripture itself. With these new views, Drummond was henceforth in hearty sympathy. His religious teaching was as much based upon the Bible as it had ever been, but in his own practical use of the Bible he exercised a new discrimination, and he often said that the critical movement had removed very many difficulties in the Old Testament which puzzled him, and had set him free for the fuller appreciation of its divine contents.

Several years afterwards, he is reported to have said:

The new view of the Bible has rendered further apologetics almost superfluous. No one now expects science from the Bible. The literary form of Genesis precludes the idea that it is science. You might as well contrast 'Paradise Lost' with geology as the Book of Genesis. The more modern views of the inspiration of the Bible have destroyed the stock-in-trade of the platform infidel.

In the Possilpark Mission, Dr Dods and Drummond shared work in those practical movements for which the religious life of Glasgow is famous, while, in Dr Dods' knowledge of literature and of the philosophical tendencies of the time, the younger man found numerous opportunities of repairing the defects in his own education.

Early in 1882 Messrs Moody and Sankey began a new mission in Scotland. The Mission was not so powerful as that of eight years before, but much real work was done.

> The inquiry room this time, as before, brings its terrible revelation of the vast multitude of unregenerate church members. I have dealt with several men of position who knew the letter of Scripture as they knew their own names, but who had no more idea of Free Grace and a Personal Christ than a Hottentot.

> I had Moody in my Church last Sabbath – one of the most wonderful meetings I ever saw …. I have been following up all week with nightly meetings.

> ~ *From letters to Robert Barbour* ~

The General Assembly of 1882 raised the mission to the status of a full charge, and Drummond resigned the missionaryship in order that an ordained minister might be appointed. This set him free to work with Mr Moody through the rest of the summer, and in October he came back to his college lectures.

During the winter he worked hard at a book, and joined Moody again for a little when the session was over. The book was the one which made him famous, *Natural Law in the Spiritual World*. It was not his greatest work. Its main argument rests upon a couple of unproved assumptions, and Drummond himself became discontented with it. But because it is still with many the chief cause of his reputation, it is right that we should form some clear idea of how this book began, and what it aimed at effecting. Drummond has himself described its origin in his Preface.

> For four years, on week days I have lectured to a class of students on the Natural Sciences, and on Sundays to an audience, consisting for

the most part of working men, on subjects of a moral and religious character. For a time I succeeded in keeping the Science and the Religion shut off from one another in two separate compartments of my mind. But gradually the wall of partition showed symptoms of giving way .... The subject-matter of Religion had taken on the method of expression of Science, and I discovered myself enunciating Spiritual Law in the exact terms of Biology and Physics.

Drummond's eyes had been opened to the great signs of evolution within Scripture itself. And on the other side, he was equally aware how Natural Science corroborates the Scriptural assumption that behind the visible universe there is a creative mind. Although he had judged Darwin's own teaching to be defective on this point, he thankfully acknowledged that Science in general bore to it unmistakable witness.

The old cry, 'How far Science has wandered away from God (Creator)', will soon be entirely obsolete, and 'How near Science has come to God' will be the watchword of the most thoughtful and far-seeing .... The first biologist in Europe [T H Huxley], when he comes to describe the development of life, can only do so in Terms of Creation. This, of course, was just what we might have expected, but I find it very remarkable that our anticipation should have been so literally fulfilled and by such authority.

~ From a letter to Hugh Barbour ~

Drummond, therefore, was never troubled by any fears that Science would contradict the fundamental postulates of the Bible on the field of the natural universe on which Science worked, and he already recognised within the historical origins of the Christian religion the same method of evolution at work as Science had recently revealed in the growth of physical life. Teachers of religion had from the very first perceived analogies or resemblances between spiritual and physical phenomena. No one, however, had proposed as yet to define these comparisons between the two sets of laws in more stringent terms. Drummond went further, and with great boldness asserted the two sets of laws to be identical.

He insisted that he arrived at this position by the inductive method, that first of all he awoke to the actual presence of certain natural laws in one department after another of the spiritual life – regeneration, growth, degeneration, and so forth. He had not first supposed his theory, and then tried if the facts would fit it, but he had first encountered the facts, gradually recognised their significance, and then deduced his general principle from them. His method, in short, had been *a posteriori*. But having thus reached his conclusions, he had found for them the corroboration of an *a priori* argument in the scientific principle of continuity.

If for nothing else than to point out the direction in which Drummond grew away from this position, it is necessary that we should here indicate the two unproved assumptions by which he reached his famous conclusion of the operation of natural law in the spiritual life. In the first place, Drummond's *a priori* argument from the principle of continuity was a huge *petitio principii*. The gulf is so great between matter and mind that the burden of proof, in the question of a continuity of law between the two, lies with him who maintains the affirmative. Drummond has simply begged the question.

And this leads us to his other unproved assumption: that, namely, in the inductive portion of his reasoning, Drummond was apparently fascinated by the use of the term 'life' to describe the phenomena in both departments without pausing to inquire whether the two kinds of life had anything more than the name in common with each other. Had he entered upon this enquiry, he must have made it obvious (as indeed it afterwards became to his own mind) that spiritual life contained elements, and was realised in conditions, so foreign to physical life that the identity of the laws governing the phenomena of both might be reasonably regarded as an impossibility.

The omission of all regard for the moral distinctions of the spiritual life is fundamental, and Drummond himself came to recognise this.

The introduction, in which these fallacies mainly enter, was not given by Drummond to his Possilpark audiences. It is a far more welcome task to turn to the great virtues of the addresses themselves. Their analysis and orderly arrangement of the facts of Christian experience, their emphasis upon the government of the religious life by law, their exposure of formalism and insincerity, conscious and unconscious, in the fashionable religion of the day, their revelation of life in Christ, their enthusiasm, their powers of practical counsel and of comfort, and their atmosphere of beauty and of peace, must have made these addresses an inspiration and a discipline of inestimable value. They have an enduring value, which not even the fallacies of the introduction to them can wholly destroy.

A month or two before Drummond's death, when he said that he wished the volume withdrawn from circulation, a friend answered, 'Remember the religious good which it has done, and is still doing, to multitudes who either never read the introduction or do not concern themselves with the philosophic questions it raises'.

Were these papers, or are such papers, even with the addition of *viva voce* explanations, not above the people? I can only say I did not find it so. My conviction, indeed, grows stronger every day that the masses require and deserve the very best work we have. The crime of evangelism is laziness, and the failure of the average mission church to reach intelligent working men rises from the indolent reiteration of threadbare formulas by teachers often competent enough, who have not first learned to respect their hearers.

... ...

I was careful in the Preface to point out the unsystematic nature of the book, but, in spite of all protest, some of my critics have searched for a philosophic or theological system, and have come back laden with spoil of every description to confound and discomfit the illogical author.

~ *From a letter to the* Clerical World ~

But for a long time Drummond was out of reach of his critics.

A few days after the publication of *Natural Law*, and before it reached the booksellers' shelves, I was steaming down the Red Sea en route for the heart of Africa.

CHAPTER 7

Diaries of Travel
1. The Rocky Mountains

HENRY Drummond made three expeditions to distant and, at the time, little-known parts of the earth: the first in 1879 to the Rocky Mountains, the second in 1883-84 to Central Africa, and the third in the summer of 1891 to the New Hebrides.

The expedition to the Rocky Mountains was a geological one, and Drummond joined it on the invitation of Sir Archibald (then Professor) Geikie, who sends the following reminiscences:

> My first acquaintance with Henry Drummond began in the University of Edinburgh at the commencement of the winter session of 1871-72. I well remember his frank, open face and the timidity of his manner as he gave his name .... I soon recognised the earnest enthusiasm and remarkable capacity of the young man. He was conspicuous by his zeal in the field, and he took a good place in the periodical examinations .... In later years, he used to come occasionally to the field excursions and he often came to consult me as to his career at College. In 1879 I planned an expedition into Western North America. Desiring a companion, I at once turned to Drummond.

[From Drummond's diary, notes on the day-to-day progress of the expedition are here omitted, but some of the most significant descriptive passages are included.]

THE CASCADES [Yellowstone]:
Water falling over a hundred little balconies, on either side these

balconies are as white as stucco. Where the cascades come down, the walls are dyed near the top a deep orange, almost red, further down a deep yellow, then saffron and exquisite shades of pink, then cream, then white. The water itself is milk-white, steaming at the top, and pattering and splashing like the fountains in gardens. The most wonderful colouring is at the south-west corner, above the petrified wood and running through it. The fountain basins here are as regular as if chiselled by hand, the colours are pink, salmon, dark and light purple, white, cinnamon.

THE [GRAND] CANYON [of the Yellowstone River]:
The most grand and memorable spectacle of my life, the inconceivable beauty and glory of the colouring, a colossal gorge zig-zagging, green, foaming, spraying, roaring river. The sides of the gorge – not clean-cut, but carved into alcoves, pinnacles, spires, of the most picturesque and fantastic forms. The original colour of the rock is pure dazzling white from river to crest, but little of the white is left save here and there a brilliant scar. The first weathering is a pale lemon yellow, deepening into saffron, sulphur, and through all the shades of yellow into the deepest orange. Then another gradation is the most tender rose-pink into vermilion and dark blood-red. The tone of the whole is a rich cream colour, deepening into russets and yellows and oranges – a kind of artificial sunlight.

GEOLOGICAL:
The rock is rhyolite – a solid mass of volcanic formation. Then the interest of the vast erosion, first of the stream, second of the weather. Great blocks of granite and gneiss are records of the glacier age. The three elements combine: fire, water, and ice.

OLD FAITHFUL [Geyser]:
At 2.20 he gave a grunt, and then threw up a little water. Visitors rushed back in alarm. Then at intervals, say at $1^1/_2$ minutes, he made another feint, then the feints became more frequent, each succeeding better than the last. Finally, he ran up 20 or 30 feet, then to the full

height. This began about 2.30, and the maximum was reached about 2.31; it remained at this height, say, one minute, and then gradually lessened.

THE MUD GEYSER:
The centre of the plate is the great scene of action. At first there lies upon it a little shape of jelly, like a custard just turned out of its cup. Suddenly it is heaved up in the air. A ragged mass of mud hangs in the air for a moment, and then as suddenly another custard is lying on the plate just like the last. Another moment of pause, the bottom of the plate is slowly knocked out once more, the custard disappears, and this time a pear lies on the plate. Then another custard, then two. Once three came all at once. There was a whole basin of these plates all going through the same legerdemain at once.

Before dinner strolled up the creek to examine *beaver-dam* more thoroughly. The dam was a sort of wickerwork, with rough big base, and more compact top of interlacing willow, mud, and stones, formed into a stiff, impervious embankment. Along the sides of the streamlet the log stumps were left standing about 2 to $2^1/_2$ feet from the ground, just gnawed off where the animal could best reach with his teeth. This dam extended far across the little valley beyond the bounds of the stream and the result was the formation of a swamp of quite considerable size. Here peat formed. The beaver as a geological agent.

Sir Archibald Geikie writes:

Drummond's singularly placid and equable temperament was like a kind of perpetual sunshine. Nothing seemed to discompose him or overshadow the winning smile that used to fascinate the wild men among whom we were thrown. And yet he was singularly impressionable. The grandeur of the scenery appealed powerfully to his imagination. He looked on everything with the eye of a poet first, and of a man of science afterwards. The human interests appealed to him before he began to dissect and compare and classify. But the marvellous interest of the geological phenomena roused his enthusiasm, sometimes to the highest pitch.

And in a letter to Professor Geikie, Drummond wrote:

The Western expedition has been a very solid gain, and I know it will be helpful to me in very many ways all my life. The whole of America impresses me now as a revelation — revelation in civilisation, in politics, in human nature, and if not a revelation in geology, a confirmation, elevation, and consolidation, which is more than equivalent.

CHAPTER 8

Diaries of Travel
2. East Central Africa

IN 1878 the African Lakes Company was formed by Glasgow gentlemen who were in sympathy with the missions, and with Livingstone's policy of developing industries for the natives.

In 1883 Mr James Stevenson FRGS was chairman of the company. It occurred to him that it would be important to have a scientific examination of the countries extending to Lake Tanganyika, and this he thought Henry Drummond could carry out. In June, Drummond went to Crieff to meet Mr Stevenson, and, leave of absence having been granted to him by the College Committee, the plan of the expedition was arranged.

Drummond kept a full journal, and also wrote regularly to his home. In *Tropical Africa* he has given a charming sketch of his travels, of the general nature of the region he crossed, and of the geological discoveries which he made upon it. [As in the previous Chapter, some descriptions are here included which may interest the modern reader.]

There is a little spring of the usual kind, bursting up among the granite pebbles, and but for its temperature and chemical composition might be one of those exquisite fountains which bubble up among the granite hills of Arran. Steam was being given off in small quantities, and a strong smell of sulphuretted hydrogen announced the presence of the mineral water at some little distance. Unfortunately, neither of my thermometers registered over 150°, so that I dared not risk them in the water. Probably Livingstone's figure, 170° Fah, expresses the exact truth. The taste reminds one of some of the home mineral waters, such as Bridge of Allan, the sulphurous taste not being disagreeably strong.

There are two characteristics of the natives. They are full of secrets. Of the white man they stand in a certain awe, which in practical matters becomes suspicion. Accordingly, they always refuse to give him information when the object for which the inquiries are asked is not perfectly patent to them. The second peculiarity is their fondness for everything in the shape of a joke.

The rock is granite (grey) and gneiss, and the geological eye is refreshed by the sight of a good honest whin dyke. It ran right up the hill, about a yard wide, with the prismatic structure well developed. The amount of basalt strewn over the hills almost surprised me. It seemed to have left its influence on the soil even more than the granite in many places where the underlying rock was undoubtedly granite. The stain of iron quite colours the soil over all these hills.

We went to sleep tonight amidst a perfect chorus of hippopotami. Their heads were rising like buoys all up and down the river – the female a red buoy, the male black. Shooting at these ironclads with any ordinary rifle is simply a waste of ammunition …. Their vocal performances are by no means musical. First, the creature slowly heaves his square skull above water and gives vent to a tremendous sniff, as if he had just caught a severe cold in the head …. He draws in air with a series of terrific grunts suggestive of a huge trombone worked by a blast furnace. The performance concludes by the creature raising himself bodily in the water almost up to the middle, and this achieved, he sinks out of sight with a sudden plunge.

My beard is now of age, and I look very old and important.

The villages are certainly unlike anything one has ever seen before. The huts are huddled together for the most part without any attempt at order, a few being reduced to something like neatness by a high stockade, which gives in the distance to the whole the appearance of an English cottage with its garden. At close quarters, however, the huts are more like the moss summer-houses one finds in country seats than human habitations. They are all of the same toadstool pattern, and miniature toadstools are often built at the side to form barns.

★   ★   ★

Dr Laws [the famous missionary] has been seven years here without a break, and much needs a holiday. The native service on Sunday was a grand sight. 500 or 600 were present, all squatting on the ground and listening with all their might. I had the pleasure of talking to them a lot, Dr Laws translating. There was also a good Sunday School, and an English service in the evening, which I took.

~ From a letter to his Father ~

★   ★   ★

A fine study in metamorphic rocks. These beds are all thin, and are pitched at a very high angle. The different rocks alternating repeatedly add considerable variety.

Scarcely two of the beds are alike. Here is a course schist [granite?] with plates of black mica three inches in length. Next it a band of most pellucid quartzite. A variegated bed of waving gneiss follows. The quartzites run through every shade from white to iron brown, one very beautiful variety being a delicate salmon pink. I describe these thus minutely, for in another year or two the geologist may look for them in vain.

Rested all day, being Sabbath. Held service in the morning with the men. They gathered in front of my door, I sitting on a box at the door. Gave out a hymn verse by verse from Dr Laws' book, three or four joining in the singing to the tune of 'Scots wha hae'. I then read the

Lord's Prayer in Chinyanja, the natives repeating as they have been taught at the Mission service. Then James ['captain' of his men] gave a short address, which I should have given a great deal to have fully understood.

The difference between the English road and the native's path is simply this – the former, made with line and level, is straight in detail, but winding as a whole. The native strikes a bee-line to his destination, but the exigencies of the case, the avoidance of trees, logs and large stones, cause it to be irregular throughout.

The rainy season is due immediately. I have enjoyed such perfect health, that I do not think it is right to run unnecessary risk. My men would suffer severely, and already many of them have had fever.

Drummond made a discovery of fossils – he believes 'the only fossils that had ever been found in Central Africa'. They lay in 'thin beds of very fine light sandstone and blue and grey shales, with an occasional band of grey limestone. Though so numerous, these fossils are confined to a single species of the "Tellinidae", a family dating back as far as the Oolites'. His journals continue:

Terrific thunderstorm with heavy rain broke out last night .... I could see from where I lay the brown torrent sweeping sticks, leaves and insects before it. The wind rose to a hurricane, and I was afraid every moment I would be unroofed.

On the newly made road, I saw at my feet a small slab of slate with markings which struck me at once as familiar. I eagerly seized it, and saw before me a fossil fish.

I felt unaccountably tired, but had no other symptom. Dr Laws insisted that I had fever. Perspiration came in an hour or two. I had no sickness, but slight oppression and headache of a new variety, though not very severe.

My fever was short-lived. – There seems now no doubt that I had a good deal of fever up-country without my knowing it. Certainly I can now account better for the want of spirit, want of appetite, laziness, weakness and general limpness which I felt so often.

Jingo [African servant] was with me to the last. I had serious thoughts of taking him home, but at last reluctantly resolved to leave him in Africa, as I felt sure he would weary away from his own tribe .... [He] was awarded first prize by universal consent .... I was really very sorry to part with poor Jingo, and he looked very lugubrious over it likewise. He came on board with me, and I took him round the great ship. He was utterly lost and bewildered, and I should give a great deal to hear his report to the natives up-country of all the wonders he saw at Quilimane.

From Quilimane Drummond sailed to East London.

In South Africa Drummond visited Lovedale, the famous mission station under Dr Stewart of the Free Church of Scotland. Cape Town was 'dirty, windy, and city-like', so he went to Wynberg 'out of sight the loveliest place I have seen in South Africa' – and spent a fortnight wandering about the base of Table Mountain.

Central Africa left a deep mark upon Drummond. He was able to give a valuable report on the geology and resources of the great country. He added infinitely to his knowledge of natural history. But it was not along any of these lines that the country left its chief influence upon him. He had revelled in his journey of exciting scenes and adventures. Then he met the first European graves. He saw missionaries laid down with fever, some suffering in solitude hundreds of miles from another white man. A white mother died in childbirth, and the only two British children in the land died. He saw, too, the Slave Trade in its most ghastly features.

Then came his own fits of lassitude and depression, attacks of fever under the pitiless rain. All this marked him for life. Although he seems to have suffered no other physical injury, there is little doubt that his spirit was affected by all he had seen and suffered.

Up till 1883 Drummond had never suffered personally. He had never known loneliness. Death had not come into his family. But in Africa he learned to know. From 1884 onwards there came upon his always pure and sympathetic temper a certain tinge of sadness. Upon his return to Scotland he said to a friend, 'I've been in an atmosphere of death all the time'.

CHAPTER 9

The Fame of Natural Law

WHILE Drummond was in Africa, his book achieved a most amazing popularity. No one was more amazed than himself. Suddenly one midnight a bundle of letters was thrust into his tent. He read that his volume had passed immediately through a first and a second edition; that the reviewers were carried away by it.

By the time Drummond reached England, the popularity had risen to fame. While some reviews disputed both its theories and conclusions, others considered it 'the most important contribution to the relations of science and religion which the country had produced'. 'A pioneer book.' 'The reader is stirred to the depths of his spiritual nature.' But not even such praise can measure the extent of its vogue among the people. Today [1899] the sales have reached 123,000 in Great Britain alone.

But the hostile criticism was repeated nowhere more persistently than in Scotland, and by none with greater conviction than by a few of the author's closest companions.

The causes of the immediate popularity of *Natural Law* are obvious. With the exception of a few passages the book is beautifully written. But the clear and simple style is charged with an enthusiasm, and carries a wealth of religious experience which capture the heart.

Among the letters which Drummond received are a large number from men and women of all degrees of culture, whose faith once strong had been shattered by the new convictions of science, and who looked for the reconciliation of the claims of science with religion, as they that look for the morning.

There were also scientific men who yearned to receive from the methods they avowed gifts to the religious side of their nature, and crowds of commonplace men and women who were in need of the pure comfort, the shrewd counsel, and the lofty ideals.

'Your book has comforted many a weary hour of my life.'
'Your book has been a benediction to me.'

Numbers traced to it their conversion from profligate lives, or from a careless and formal Christianity.

An Anglican divine said it was the best book he had ever read upon the Christian experience.

Another theologian wrote: 'I feel that you have added enormously to the avenues of my own spiritual existence.'

One of the foremost authorities in his own branch of science wrote: 'Long pondering has led me through much difficulty and doubt and pain to see the matter just as you see it .... I believe your book will be of inestimable value to many a troubled and distracted soul .... I do not know any thoughtful agnostic who does not doubt his own conclusions. Such a book as yours will appeal with great force to all such.'

Of a different class are those who claim Drummond's adhesion to their own denomination or particular heresy. Perhaps the greatest number of letters came from promoters of the application to the future life of the doctrine of 'the survival of the fittest'. Then the foes of 'Bibliolatry' congratulate him on having removed religion from a Scriptural basis.

Many blame him for not settling all the great problems of religion and life. The same questions followed Drummond wherever he lectured during the next ten years – the Atonement, free-will, the gift of free grace, why Jesus was a Jew.

Reasonable objections to *Natural Law* were formulated in serious articles and pamphlets, which, though they are in the main hostile, bear unmistakable tribute to the impression made by the book.

But *Natural Law* encountered more than criticism of this honest and able kind. It roused both the '*odium theologicum*' and that which is scarcely less savage, the '*odium scientificum*'. Many [evangelicals] withdrew from religious associations of which he was a member, they would not speak from the same platform, they published pamphlets against him, and wrote him bitter and contemptuous letters. They said: 'He founds religion upon science, and to do so is to be an infidel.' One religious paper gave orders to its reporters at a large convention in America not to take down anything that Henry Drummond might say. His services as an evangelist, the great amount of positive Christian doctrine that he taught, were ignored by these hunters of a fancied heresy. They would have been (from their own point of view) more profitably occupied in proving it a fallacy. But this none of them seemed to see.

Drummond met all attacks upon him with great good temper; one never heard him say a word against the most violent of his opponents.

The book appears to have excited the greatest attention in Germany, Scandinavia and Russia. The criticism of theologians is summed up by Dr Otto Zockler:

One may grant that the criticism of Drummond has given expression to much that is correct. Such an acknowledgement, however, must not mislead us into ignoring the healthy stimulus which has proceeded from Drummond's writings. If several English critics have complained of Drummond's 'evolutionist gospel' as scarcely different from ordinary Darwinism, there is not only strong exaggeration in such a complaint, but also disregard of the fact that the Glasgow scholar has several times expressed himself – especially in *The Ascent of Man* – against the unlimited validity of the Darwinian principle of the 'Struggle for Existence'.

CHAPTER 10

Evolution and Revelation

THE extract below comes from two articles by Henry Drummond in *The Expositor* for 1885, soon after his return from Africa.

On bare facts science from first to last is based. Now if Christianity possesses anything, it possesses facts. So long as the facts were presented to the world, Christianity spread with marvellous rapidity. But there came a time when the facts were less exhibited to men than the evidence for the facts. Theology, that is to say, began to rest upon authority ....

[Looking at facts] is the method of all Reformation; it was the method of *the* Reformation. Now Christianity is learning from science to go back to its facts ....

The evidence for Christianity is not the Evidences. The evidence for Christianity is a Christian. The natural man, his regeneration by the Holy Spirit, the spiritual man and his relations to the world and to God, these are the modern facts for a scientific theology ....

But not less essential, in the scientific method, than the examination of facts is the arrangement of them under laws. And the work of modern science has resulted in its demonstration of the uniformity of nature ....

There may be laws, or actings, in the spiritual world which it may seem to some impossible to include in such a scheme. God is not, in theology, a Creator merely, but a father. He may act in different cases in different ways. This is the law of the Father, the law of free-will; it is the law of all fathers, of all free-wills. Into ordinary family relations science rarely feels called to intrude; in dealing with this class of cases in the spiritual world, science is attempting a thing which in the natural world it leaves alone ....

Science is nothing if not practical, and the scientific method has little for Christianity after all if it is not to enrich the lives of its followers. It is worth while, therefore, taking a single example of its practical value ....

There is nothing more appalling than the wholesale way in which unthinking people plead to the Almighty for the richest and most spiritual of his promises without themselves fulfilling one of the conditions on which they can possibly be given ....

And science could make no truer contribution to modern Christianity than to enforce upon us all the law of causation in spiritual life. The reason why so many people get nothing from prayer is that they expect effects without causes, and this also is the reason why they give it up. It is not irreligion that makes men give up prayer, but the uselessness of their prayers ....

Danger arises, not from the use of the scientific method, but from its use apart from the scientific spirit .... And as science can help Christianity with the former, Christianity may perhaps do something for science as regards the latter ....

The haste to be wise, like the haste to be rich, can only end in fallen fortunes. The one safeguard is to use the intellectual method in sympathetic association with the moral spirit ....

Let us now consider one or two of the achievements [of the scientific method]. We should be wrong to look to it for any very pronounced contribution as yet to the higher truths of religion .... We should go back at once to Genesis, and expect the first serious contribution to theology on the doctrine of creation.

And what do we find? Science comes to us not only freighted with vast treasures of newly noticed facts, but with a theory which by many thoughtful minds has been accepted as the method of creation. And more than this, it tells us candidly that it has failed to discover any clue to the ultimate mystery of origins, any clue which can compete

Henry Drummond

Drummond's parents and their family

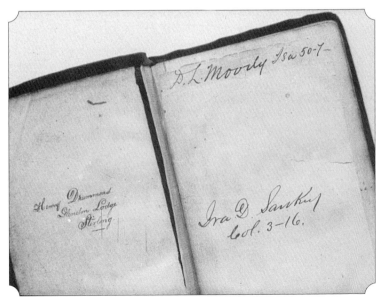

Drummond's New Testament with signatures of Moody and Sankey

Drummond in his study

'Glenelm', Stirling

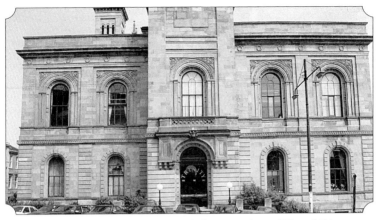

Free Church College, Glasgow where he became Professor of Natural Science

HENRY DRUMMOND
BORN · 27TH · JULY 1809 · DIED · 1ST JAN · 1888
HIS · WIFE
JANE · CAMPBELL · BLACKWOOD
BORN · 1ST · AUGUST · 1825 · DIED · 20TH · AUGUST · 1910
AND · THEIR · SONS
FREDERICK · DIED · 30TH · NOV · 1862 · AGED · 5 · YEARS
HENRY · DRUMMOND · F·R·S·E· F·G·S
PROFESSOR · OF · NATURAL · SCIENCE
FREE · CHURCH · COLLEGE · GLASGOW
BORN · 17TH · AUG · 1851 · DIED · 11TH · MARCH · 1897

Drummond headstone in churchyard of the Holy Rude, Stirling with the view of theology …. Science has not found a substitute for God.

It says: 'The atheist tells us there is nothing there. We cannot believe him. We cannot tell what it is, but there is certainly something. Agnostics we may be, we can no longer be atheists' ….

Science offers to theology a doctrine of the method of creation in its hypothesis of evolution. That this doctrine is proved yet, no one will assert. That in some of its forms it is never likely to be proved, many are convinced. Yet it fills a gap at the very beginning of our religion. Science has supplied theology with a theory which the intellect can accept, and which for the devout mind leaves everything more worthy of worship than before ….

According to science, evolution is the method of creation. Now creation is a form of revelation. If, then, science were to be told of another revelation – an inspired word – it would expect that this other revelation would also be an evolution ….

Now if science searches the field of theology for an additional revelation, it will find a Bible awaiting it – a Bible in two forms. The one is the Bible as it was presented to our forefathers, the other is the Bible of modern theology. To science the difference is immediately palpable. The one represents revelation as having been produced on the Divine – fiat hypothesis, the other on the slow-growth or evolution theory ….

Theology no more pledges itself today to the interpretations of the Bible of 1000 years ago, than does science to the interpretations of nature in the time of Pythagoras ….

The supreme contribution of Evolution to Religion is that it has given us a clearer Bible. There are many things in the Bible which are hard to reconcile with our ideas of a just and good God. But these difficulties arise simply from an old-fashioned or unscientific view of what the Bible is. We see now that the mind of man has been slowly developing, and that revelation has been adapted to the successive stages through which that development has passed ….

Evolution has given to theology a vastly more reasonable body of truth about God and man …. Evolution has given Christianity a new

Bible .... The Bible is not a book which has been made; it has grown. Hence it is no longer a mere word-book, nor a compendium of doctrines, but a nursery of growing truths ....

It may be said that the Christian does not need a transformed Bible. But Theology is only beginning to realise how radical is the change in mental attitude of those who have learned to think from science .... They have studied the facts, they have looked with their own eyes at what God did, and they are giving us a book which is more than the devout man's Bible. It is the apologist's Bible ....

Such a Bible cannot be proclaimed to the mass of the people too soon. It is no more fair to brandish objections to the Bible without studying carefully what scientific theologians have to say on the subject, than it would be fair for one who derived his views of the natural world from Pythagoras to condemn all science .... When science makes its next attack on theology, it will find an armament, largely furnished by itself, which has made the Bible as impregnable as nature ....

It is certain that every step of science discloses the attributes of the Almighty with a growing magnificence.

In 1886 Drummond wrote for the *Nineteenth Century* a short article entitled 'Mr Gladstone and Genesis'. William Gladstone and T H Huxley had been waging a controversy upon the relations between the teaching of Genesis and that of modern science upon the creation or evolution of life.

On the one side, Drummond accepted Mr Huxley's statement that it is impossible to harmonise Genesis and science; on the other side, he denied that the contradiction between them was fatal to the belief that Genesis contains 'a revelation of truth from God'.

There was no science then. Scientific questions were not even asked then .... Doubtless there are valid reasons why the Bible does not contain a technological dictionary and a pharmacopoeia, or anticipate the *Encyclopaedia Britannica*. But that it does not inform us on practical matters is surely a valid argument why we should not expect it to instruct the world in geology ....

Genesis is a presentation of one or two great elementary truths to the childhood of the world. A scientific theory of the universe formed no part of the original writer's intention. The object is purely religious, the point being not how things were made, but that God made them. It is not dedicated to science, but to the soul ....

Nature in Genesis has no link with geology and needs none. Man has no link with biology, and misses none. What he really needs and really misses, Genesis gives him; it links nature and man with their Maker. The scientific man must go there to complete his science. What is really there he cannot attack, for he cannot do without it. Nor let religion plant positions there which can only keep science out. Then only can the interpreters of Nature and the interpreters of Genesis understand each other.

From all this, it is apparent how far Drummond had travelled from the positions of the older orthodoxy which he described in the college essay, quoted in Chapter Three. To question them seemed to many to be treason; to abandon them madness. But Drummond was forced from them by his study of natural science and of Biblical criticism and Biblical theology. And upon the new positions to which he was led, he has evidently found a basis for his faith more stable than ever the older was imagined to be – richer mines of Christian experience and truth, better vantage grounds for preaching the Gospel of Christ, and loftier summits with infinitely wider prospects of the power of God, and of the destiny of man.

CHAPTER 11

1884-1890

B Y 260 votes to 167 the General Assembly of 1884 'enacted and ordained that the Theological Faculty of Glasgow shall consist of five professors instead of four, the additional professor being a professor of Natural Science'.

On 31 May Drummond was unanimously elected to the new Chair, and the Assembly instructed the Presbytery of Glasgow to arrange for his 'ordination and induction'. This took place on 4 November in College Free Church, according to the simple Scottish rite, and by laying on of the hands of the Presbytery.

(Probably Drummond had been anxious not to be ordained as a full minister of the Church, for after the ordination and to the end of his life, he persisted – to the amusement of his friends – that he had never been ordained as a minister. The fact, however, is beyond all doubt. He received the full orders of the Presbyterian Church.)

The Reverend George Reith, in delivering the charge, said: 'A professor is all the better for having known the practical work of the ministry, and in your case, though the name has been wanting, the thing has been there. We look to you as one especially qualified to show how culture and sympathy with evangelistic work are to go hand in hand.'

Professor Drummond then delivered his inaugural address on the 'Contribution of Science to Christianity', virtually the same as the articles in the *Expositor,* quoted in the previous Chapter.

To James Stevenson [who funded the new chair]:
I believe in the work of this chair more and more every day. Indeed, perhaps it is due to you that I should tell you what I have not told anyone here, that I lately refused a very lucrative Government appointment lest it should hinder me in my new work.

The course through which Drummond took his class continued to be the same as it had been. He lectured four hours a week, and besides expounding the principles of modern science and their relation to religion, taught the elements of botany and geology, and, I believe, a little zoology. An 'old student' wrote:

Once a week he used to give his class special lectures, beginning with the evolution of the world, and coming down to the evolution of life. These were intensely interesting, and were more useful than the mere teaching of the rudiments of science.

Drummond welcomed his work in the College for the time which it left him to minister to a far wider congregation in the matters of morality and religion. Of this ministry an enormous increase was brought to him by the fame of his book. Yet, having read his African journal, one is tempted to regret that he did not spend a quiet year in elaborating the results of his travels into a careful treatise upon the geology and resources of the Zambezi and Nyasa regions.

Henry spoke to us tonight on Paul's Hymn of Heavenly Love in the thirteenth of First Corinthians, and it was like being in heaven or in sight of it to hear him …. He is hesitating whether to give some time to rigorous scientific work, as a monograph on some of his African spoils, or whether to go in entirely for evangelism. I think the latter will have it.

~ *From a letter of Robert W Barbour* ~

The latter did have it, and could not but have it. The author of

Natural Law in the Spiritual World was bound to be sought after by the more religious portions of what is termed 'Society'. Our national life is probably nowhere so sensitive to influence as throughout its upper ranks, and the individuals who had been benefited by Drummond busied themselves to extend the boon throughout their class. Among the new friends found by Drummond were Lord and Lady Aberdeen, with whom his relations for the rest of his life were most close and affectionate.

> I should really have some faith in addresses of a simple kind – not written lectures, but clear statements of what Christianity really is.
>
> *~ From a letter to the Earl of Aberdeen ~*

Drummond agreed to give three addresses in the ballroom of Grosvenor House, London:

> The first day the place was filled, and none were turned away. The second, another room was thrown open. There is no service – just an address for an hour. The room was full of members of the Upper House. They came expecting to hear a lecture on science, but Henry took the simplest evangelical subject he could – about Conversion. It is a wonderful opportunity God is giving him, and he is wonderfully fitted for it.
>
> *~ From a letter of Robert W Barbour ~*

To be able to collect on successive Sunday afternoons 400 or 500 people, many of them of the highest distinction, social and intellectual, is a triumph of ingenuity. Mr Drummond has invented a gospel which, if not entirely new, has just enough novelty about it to interest the fashionable public. He applies the law of the survival of the fittest to spiritual existence. He does not consign to perdition all who fail to lead a highly spiritual life here. He only reminds them that they are not qualifying themselves for the life to come …. The audience has departed profoundly impressed by the words of wisdom and solemnity issuing from the lips of a young man with a good manner, a not ill-favoured face, a broad Scotch accent, clad in a remarkably well-fitting frock-coat. Mr Drummond has, in fact, produced upon his hearers the impression that the teachings of science are, upon the whole, in favour of revealed religion ....

The Church papers hint that he is an amateur and a quack. But then that is only professional jealousy. It is enough to observe that audiences, as fastidious and discriminating and as highly educated as any in the world, have been won over by his utterances. He has caused society to talk not only about himself, but about the subjects which he expounds.

~ From The World, *May 1889 ~*

A letter from Drummond himself reports the beginning of an effort to organise women of the West End of London into an Associated Workers' League for social and religious help among the poor. By 1890 the total membership was 240. Reports were periodically asked from workers, and the endeavour was made to inspire in the members 'the true temper of work, as distinct from mere busyness in good works'.

To Drummond, the year 1886 was to bring many changes and many cares. In February the political life of the nation was convulsed by Mr Gladstone's declaration of a policy of Home Rule for Ireland. The Earl of Aberdeen was appointed Viceroy of Ireland, and offered Henry Drummond a post on his staff. In his reply he said, 'Now I am not sure that it would be right for me to do this – right in connection with one's real work and mission in life. If I could be of real use in the more official capacity, that of course would weigh, but I can be of none, and I am fearful lest I injure any evangelistic work that may be given to me to do'.

Drummond adhered to the portion of the Liberal Party which followed Mr Gladstone. In such opinions Drummond was fortified by his recent visit to Ireland and his experience of the effect upon the people of the reign of a Viceroy who represented a Government pledged to Home Rule. So he was not only prepared to give his vote for this at the coming election, but to speak in public on its behalf with conviction, and even with enthusiasm.

Drummond was urgently requested to stand for several constituencies, but he refused to launch upon a line of life which would have distracted him from the vocation that he felt, and had now so amply proved, to be his own.

I feel that I can serve you and the great cause better in other ways than by myself entering Parliament …. I believe that, by working in the fixed walk of life which seems to be assigned to me, I can do more for every cause of truth and righteousness.

~ From a letter to the Right Honourable William E Gladstone ~

But while refusing to stand for any constituency, Drummond gave help to several Liberal candidates, and he did not appear on those political platforms without the same kind of preparation that he invariably made for his religious addresses.

Drummond went to Switzerland with his sisters for part of September.

There is but one spot in the world, and its name is Axenstein. The scenery is of the very noblest type, with views everywhere of the most bewildering beauty and sublimity.

~ From a letter to Lady Aberdeen ~

Drummond stayed on in Switzerland to prepare addresses to German universities [including Tübingen and Bonn].

By November 2 he was in Glasgow, and 'in a whirl of work'.

Look at the queer stamp on the outside of this letter. As Viceroy (temporarily Ex.) I thought you might like to see the new symbols of the Crown …. I do not know if you have a weakness for stamps, but I confess this relic of boyhood still survives in me.

~ From a letter to Lord Aberdeen ~

On Sunday week the students open a campaign among the bigger Edinburgh schoolboys. We have got athletic men, whom the schoolboys all know, to take this in hand.

What it is exactly that travel gives, and is, one can scarcely define, though not the least of it must be the immensely bigger environment to *think* in .... In Edinburgh the current is flowing deep and strong. I do not think I would exchange that audience for anything else in the world.

Moody writes urgently about going to America for a students' gathering, and I think I must go.

~ From letters to Lady Aberdeen ~

Drummond's work in America was among the colleges, and falls to be described in another Chapter. He returned to find his father dangerously ill.

How suddenly the water deepens sometimes in one's life. Well, I suppose it must be better, this deeper sea, than the shallows where the children play .... One thing I am learning, slowly, to believe in prayer.

The thing that crushes is to look on silently at the unalleviable pain of those we love. But God knows the end; and it is His natural order that generation after generation should pass away.

What an entrancing thing Death is! I am glad I am an evolutionist. Yet its surroundings are very terrible.

Trouble is not such a new thing to you. But it is to me .... The great benediction of it seems to lie less in the personal elements than in the larger views one gets of what is permanent, eternal, and most worth living for. My father lived for these things if ever a man did.

31 December. Nun Gott sei mit, durch dieses Jahr! And please see the blue in the sky, and there is always more than we can see.

1 January 1888. My father passed away this morning at five o'clock. You did not know him, but he was a good soldier.

~ From letters to a Friend watching beside her Mother's bed ~

The winter and spring of 1888 were spent by Drummond on his college class, and on what had now become his yearly meetings for the Edinburgh students. There was the usual visit to Arran with his students in the end of March.

On the Higher Education of Women, he writes to Lady Aberdeen:

The main thing surely is that it be *real,* and not the new accretion of further 'accomplishments'. *Wise* women, balanced women, are what are needed, not accomplished ornaments – or bores. Specifically then, they should be educated to be E. *women* and not second-rate E. *men.* The three things they should know from the foundation to the top are: (Mind) Education (What? Why? How?), (Body) Physiology and Ethics, Psychology and (Soul) Theology.'

In May Drummond received a remarkable requisition to deliver another series of religious addresses at Grosvenor House during the London season.

I am strongly of opinion that only *three* addresses, and on the Sundays you name, should be announced. When a long series is intimated, men imagine they can go at any time, and a main object should be to keep the first day's audience through the course rather than to have new men coming in at the end. An isolated address is almost useless.

I am quite at a loss for the title of my subject. Would it do to name no subject? I fear no title would quite cover the ground one would like to go over.

~ From a letter to Captain Sinclair, who acted as Secretary ~

The great square room was crowded by politicians, clergymen, authors, artists, critics, soldiers and barristers, with a large sprinkling of smart young men, whose appearance could scarcely have suggested a vivid interest in serious concerns.

~ From the Pall Mall Gazette *~*

The addresses (I do not know in what order) were on 'Evolution and Christianity', 'Natural Selection in Reference to Christianity', and 'The Programme of Christianity'.

Professor Drummond said that the truth of Christianity is manifest in the fact that there is no real civilisation without it …. He showed its adaptability to the most pressing requirements of the individual and of society, accounted for its apparent failure to accomplish its mission by the unfaithfulness of Christians to their own ideal, and compared the efficacy of Christ's Gospel in ministering to such common ills as poverty, distress, melancholy, and bad habits, with that of Socialism, Political Economy, and Natural Morality ….

Illustrating the meaning of the term 'survival of the fittest' by the case of the tadpole, Professor Drummond said that when they came to religion they found the same state of matters. Those who had here, in their being, somewhere, an apparatus for living in an unseen environment would survive, because they were fit, and not because they were worthy of eternal life ….

God had invited every man and woman to come to Him that they might have life, and if they resisted that invitation, it looked as if the chance diminished every year of life.

It was a question of the survival of the fittest. This was not an arbitrary enactment on God's part. It was a natural selection of those who had become fit ….

It was not religiousness nor good works that constituted fitness. It was the possession of the mind of Christ …. All men could be eligible if they would get into the environment suitable to the development of this fitness …. There was an undeveloped bud in every man, and they had only to abide in Christ, and it would grow into beauty.

~ From a newspaper report ~

Drummond addressed a large meeting of young women in the residence of the Speaker of the House of Commons. This meeting was held in pursuance of the aims of the Associated Workers' League started in 1885, and a separate club was formed from among those present for the purpose of informing and guiding them in all the usual work to which they had given themselves .... 'to make service for others the aim of our lives'.

> The change from London has been delightful. I have had four days' absolute peace and indolence. Yesterday I had a service at 12 in the servants' hall, to which keepers, foresters, and their wives trooped in for miles and miles, and I liked the thing much better than Grosvenor House.
>
> *~ From a letter written at Lochmore Lodge, Lairg ~*

In the middle of August, Drummond started for a tour.

> I am lost in wonder all day long. Switzerland is the one place in the world which is never false to old impressions.
>
> *~ From a letter from Engelberg, Switzerland ~*

> I met Browning today and had a chat; also the Queen of Portugal – and had no chat.
>
> *~ From a letter from Venice ~*

(He had met Robert Browning in 1885, when he wrote: 'He is quite unlike a poet, and talks plain prose. To meet him, you would think he was an elderly but well-preserved and smart French banker.')

The winter of 1888-89 passed in the usual labours – college lectures, new addresses for Edinburgh, and endless meetings of philanthropic societies. Claim after claim upon him had to be refused in the interests of his work for his students. Part of his work this year was the founding of a University Settlement in Glasgow. His intense interest at this time in such work is proof of how far he had advanced in his conception of Christianity since the early days, when the social side of religion had few charms for him.

In April, Dr Smeaton, Professor of New Testament Exegesis in New College, Edinburgh, died, and Drummond threw himself into the work of securing the election of Dr Dods to the vacant chair.

The young men are rallying finely, and the issue is now seen to be the large question of Liberalism versus Toryism. I have long wanted a test vote on that point, as Scotland has changed much even since Robertson Smith was put out. Many good people must pass through tribulation – the price of progress.

~ From a letter to Lady Aberdeen ~

Holiness is an infinite compassion for others: Greatness is to take the common things of life and walk truly among them: Happiness is a great love and much serving.

~ Quoted in a letter to a Friend ~

I wonder if you feel, as I do, an unhealthy liking for *new* books. I have continually to pull myself up and go back to old and dusty friends – to find them after all the best.

A *Nineteenth Century* article should be written at least three times – once in simplicity, once in profundity, and once to make the profundity appear simplicity.

Dresden? Freut mich sehr to hear you speak of it. All I have heard of it is good, and you will get what you need most just now – art, both music and painting. You must read the Masters a bit between this and then. How I wish I could do that!

I tried everywhere for a bound copy of *Greatest Thing*, but it was nowhere to be found, and no copies are yet forthcoming.

~ From other letters to Friends ~

Drummond did not do his publishing like other authors. He chose paper, type and binding, and dealt with the printers himself. He said he enjoyed the 'sport' of it.

Invitations reached Drummond from the Australian colleges to come and tell them of the Edinburgh Student Movement, and do what he had done in America. He had refused to go to Australia the year before, but now he agreed.

> I am taking Browning complete [to read on the voyage]. None can approach him for insight into life, or even into Christianity .... I have to introduce into Australia the Boys' Brigade, the Home Reading Union, and other modern improvements.

> ~ *From letters to Lady Aberdeen* ~

1884-1890 – These seven years of Drummond's life were the years of his fame and greatest activity along many lines. Even in them he did nothing greater than his work among students. To follow the movement we must return to 1884, in which year it started in Edinburgh.

CHAPTER 12

The Student Movement 1884-1894

BESIDES his mission to young men under Mr Moody, the greatest work which Henry Drummond achieved was his work among students. Started at Edinburgh in 1884, it spread to many other colleges of Great Britain. It took him to Germany, to America and to Australia. Up to the very end it remained his chief interest and burden.

He shut himself off from the pulpits of his Church, denied his friends, turned from the public, banished reporters, and endured infinite misrepresentation, if only he might make sure of the students. Measured by results, almost everything else he did seems less; for the field was one on which other ministers of religion had many failures, and he conspicuously succeeded. He invented methods that are now employed whenever students join for religious service. He preached the Gospel of Christ with a fullness and with a pertinacity of personal application which he never excelled on any other platform. And so he influenced thousands of lives which are now at work among many nations.

In December 1884 Drummond made his first appearance before his own university as a teacher by giving the annual lecture of its Christian Medical Association. His audience saw before them a religious teacher utterly free from conventionalism, loyal to the intellectual methods of the age, but with an unshaken faith in God and in the reality of spiritual experience. He was urged to return and lead the movement which had just started. The Oddfellows' Hall was chosen, and the audience nearly filled the hall.

One who was present says: 'He proceeded to enforce on them the command of Jesus, "Seek ye first the Kingdom of God and His righteousness". He intimated that an after-meeting would be held. No urgent appeal was made; rather they were told that probably the best thing for some of them would be to go home and speak with none but God. Yet the after-meeting was large.'

With one break, Drummond returned every Sunday evening till the end of the session.

> You have come to Edinburgh, some of you from the ends of the earth, to learn. You matriculated; and becoming a University student, you went to get from each individual professor what he had to teach. So, with definite purpose to learn of Christ, must you come to Him and surrender yourself to His teaching and guidance.

Even with his experience of such movements, Drummond was taken by surprise. 'It is a distinct work of God,' he writes, 'such a work as I have never seen before.'

He refused invitations to visit other universities; but these of themselves seemed ready for the movement, and from Edinburgh deputations were sent to address meetings. In Aberdeen, from about 800 students, 380 attended the first meeting, more than 300 the second and third.

In Glasgow, the movement was still stronger.

> The hall was crowded to excess by the most orderly students' meeting I ever attended. There were many cases of true conversion, and also of spiritual quickening. Dr McKendrick [who presided] told me the meeting was the finest he had ever attended.
>
> ~ *From a letter to James M Macphail, then a Medical Student* ~

Though Drummond could not attend any of those Sunday meetings, he met with the Glasgow students on week-days for prayer and conference.

Which of us does not remember the advent of the first 'Holiday

Missioners' among our manses? They were sent, not as advocates, but as witnesses, and they gave their testimonies with freshness and simplicity. They had little or no theology, but they told of Christ's power upon themselves. They talked too of their doubts and intellectual difficulties in a way that proved very profitable to us ministers in dealing with young men. They interested us greatly by their open reflection of Drummond. His way of putting things, his stories, his accent, his characteristic reserve, his pauses and hesitations were reproduced almost to mimicry. It was a great tribute to the influence of his personality; but how we used to chaff him about it!

The organisation of the Holiday Mission cost Drummond and his assistants very much thought and hard work. He knew the perils to which his young missioners were exposed, and both received reports on the conduct of each, and returned frank warnings.

In October 1885 Drummond made his mission to the undergraduates of Oxford. The proposal for this had begun with some of his hearers at Grosvenor House, and with one or two Oxford heads who had read his book.

I am given to understand that the various parties [High Church and Low Church] are not nearly so distinct and alien as they were some years ago, and that a combined evangelistic work is not impossible ….

When I got to Trinity, the door being blocked, they were pouring in through the windows and filling every inch of space. I need not say how inspiring this sight was. It was a most unconventional and picturesque audience – the thing I liked best …. They are in danger of many things, especially cant and too aggressive evangelism. I am going to douse them with cold water this afternoon.

I gave them a sketch of the Edinburgh movement. They seemed much surprised at our views, but did not instantly burn me at the stake, as I feared. I had no idea it would be part of my work here to run a tilt at the evangelism in the place …. The time is not ripe yet, there are not the men to do it. In fact I feel this week more like reconnoitring than doing the actual battle – that must be done by somebody later.

I called for Dean Liddell yesterday on his granting the hall at Christchurch. He gave me pretty clearly to understand that it was solely on Aberdeen's account. He thawed a little after twenty minutes over tea, but I thought him very appalling ....

I have told the Low Church men to keep out of sight. To them our ways of work, our leading ideas, the absence of cant, and of evangelical formulas are a complete revelation, and I really think they will adopt them .... The High Church party have arranged a special series of University sermons, and have engaged some splendid men .... It would be a real gain to unite the low and high factions in a piece of neutral evangelistic work.

~ From letters to Lady Aberdeen ~

We had a tremendous turnout at All Souls College; in fact, as the Americans say, it was necessary to take the paper off the walls. I am at it every night this week. I think the place is ripe.

~ From a letter to Professor Greenfield [Glasgow] *~*

If Drummond was right – and he was an expert in the work – there was nobody and nothing at Oxford to reap the harvest. Men of all religious schools had been impressed by Drummond's addresses and his explanation of the methods on which he worked, but insuperable differences of opinion were revealed as to methods. These were not differences between Church and Dissent, but between High and Low Church. The work was abandoned.

In Glasgow no movement arose, growing and permanent, like the movement in Edinburgh, and in subsequent years Drummond does not appear to have tried to start one. Those Glasgow students who are most interested in religion are occupied with city missions, in which they have an amount of work and responsibility that effectually disables them from other interests.

In Edinburgh the movement continued and increased, and Drummond went back for another series of meetings in February and March 1886.

> I have been trying to tell them something about the Kingdom of God …. A desire has sprung up to have the Sacrament all together …. Tonight we have a meeting to organise the Summer Holiday Mission. Belfast and the North of Ireland are to have strong deputations in April ….
>
> I am starting now to see the International Football Match at Edinburgh.

The secretary of the Holiday Mission reported in April 1886 deputations to between 15 and 20 places in Scotland, England, Wales and Ireland. Most important was the work at Aberystwyth, and Drummond himself went to it.

> For two days the students from Edinburgh held no meetings at all, but attended the Annual Athletic Sports of the University, and otherwise threw themselves into the students' interests. The effect of this was to secure the whole 'varsity' for the meeting on Wednesday, and a profound impression it made.
>
> *~ From a letter to Lord Aberdeen from Aberystwyth ~*

The difficulties were great, chiefly the jealousies between Church and Chapel, but the work progressed and spread.

During the summer Professor Christlieb wrote from Bonn, inviting a deputation of students to come over. *Natural Law* had been translated into German, and Drummond's name was well known.

But from Bonn Drummond wrote: 'The difficulties here are enormous. Evangelism is hated, loathed. Still a feeble spark may smoulder on.'

Back in Glasgow, he wrote: 'I have only time to say one word about Bonn. It was a strange experience. The chief feature of the mission was one big meeting. Questions were invited at the end. The depth of ignorance shown in these questions was appalling.'

But Drummond must have made a deep impression at Bonn, for among his papers I find an invitation from a large body of students to return.

Dec. 16. For me it will be a quiet winter. I have begun *The Ascent of Man,* though it climbs slowly, slowly. Then after the Christmas holidays I begin Edinburgh. I have purposely left it alone this month to let them try themselves. And they have succeeded perfectly.

Mar. 3, 1887. The Boys' Meeting also, which was meant to last a Sunday or two, has grown into an institution, and will not stop .... One difficulty is to get into their heads that they are to be religious *as boys,* and that they need not be so 'pious' as their maiden aunts.

Mar. 24. Sunday was our last great meeting for the winter, and I can never forget it. Our hall was crammed to the door, and at the close we asked all the men who had become Christians to remain and join in the Sacrament. Over 600 waited – men of every kindred and tongue.

Mar. 31. I take my students for a week's geology in Arran every year, and I cannot tell you what a relief it is to get out of the smoke ....

Edinburgh still glows. We have not been able to stop the meetings. I had four last Sunday, and have four more next.

So from year to year the work went on. The summer and autumn of 1887 saw it carried by Drummond himself to the American Universities, as will be described in another chapter. When he returned to Scotland, he found the Edinburgh students as eager as ever, and the arrival of a deputation from America gave the movement a new impulse.

January 28, 1888. Did you see a letter in the *Christian* about my heresies? A small clique has addressed a printed circular to the

Edinburgh ministers, begging them to suppress me and my views. Of course, I have taken no notice, and I think it has not hindered the work at all, which is the main thing …. I have an important commission for ———— to rush a Bill through Parliament securing a Copyright in Public Speech: *ie,* to prevent these irresponsible miscreants, the reporters, from doing their work except when permission and revision are granted by their miserable victims.

March 26, 1888. It is very hard to be called names, but very right, and in the nature of things altogether inevitable. 'It is enough for the servant that he be as his Master.'

In session 1888-89 it was still the same. And session 1889-90 saw the work as engrossing as in previous years.

January 6, 1890. It is the busiest time amongst the poor, and especially among the tempted, and it has fallen to my lot this year to devote my holiday mainly to them, turning up at my mother's from time to time as I could.

Drummond's notes for the years 1884-90 hold good also for 1891-94. In these ten years the work covered three generations of students, and Drummond was able to give many of his better-known addresses more than once, but always with varieties and additions suitable to the occasion.

At first his addresses were all upon the relation of the individual to Christ. In 1886 he began to emphasise the social aspects of religion, and gave some addresses on the Kingdom of God, based on Isaiah 61 and I Corinthians 13. Then, while preparing his lectures on *The Ascent of Man,* he took up the relations of science and religion, and illustrated the naturalness of Christianity as the crown of all human evolution, but always drove home to the individual his place and duty in the process.

Take the very remarkable series of addresses delivered in the winter of 1890. Modern science has enabled him to view life as a whole, and to perceive that in the universe Christianity is at once the most natural and the most sublime of facts. He sweeps before us the forces which have built the world, developed the individual, and fashioned human society, and he relates Christianity to them as their continuance and consummation. There is no sensation in the addresses, nor any imposition of authority, no artificiality nor false mysticism, but the style is as simple as the thinking, it is one sensible man talking to others of his own generation.

In the Christianity which he presents, Jesus Christ is the Source of all life and light; the assurance of forgiveness of sins; the daily nourishment of the soul, the one power sufficient for a noble life; the solution of all problems; the motive and example of all service. The Bible and Christ's own words are expounded with a simplicity that reminds one sometimes of Luther. Church-going, Drummond says, is not Christianity, and belief in doctrine is not Christianity, but no sane man will refuse the regular nourishment and strength of fellowship which church-going supplies, and, as in every department of science, so here also a reasonable mind will recognise that there must be doctrines, and will go for their explanation to the highest authorities.

Nor will he who reads these addresses need to be told how ignorant and irrelevant was the criticism from which their author suffered. Some of the misrepresentations were wilful, others were the effect of the inevitable distortion of the half-reported teaching of an evangelist with unconventional ways of stating the truth. In fact, when Drummond's harder critics went to hear him, they generally came away disarmed.

Professor Drummond spoke with evident earnestness, but with marked control, if not reserve. His whole bearing was calm and collected. There were no gestures. Nor was there a suggestion of the 'preacher' – natural voice, natural demeanour, natural and dignified from beginning to end ....

He had a most exceptional faculty of simple, beautiful and dignified expression. I had heard a real *Teacher*. Such are rare. Many professors in our universities can no more teach than fly! At best, possibly they are crammers-in. But Drummond *e*-ducated men. He drew them out – and drew them onwards and upwards ....

He had a greater and more lasting effect upon the University at that time than any of the University teachers themselves. And for a very simple reason. He dealt not with technical subjects, but with ethics and life. He went beneath the surface of things beyond formularies, creeds, definitions – to the elementary questions of life and conduct. I should sum up his entire teaching in one sentence of George MacDonald: 'Life and religion are one thing, or neither is anything.' Here was a minimum of theology and a maximum of simple common sense ....

Nor was the effect immediately transient. It acted in a perceptible measure as the salt of the University. The foremost men in the University gave these meetings their support, and were often present themselves ....

The final result was a revealing of unity, co-ordination and adaptation in the Truth of the Christian Religion and Nature. Nature was to Drummond a sympathetic background to human life and the kindred revelation of a divine intelligence .... He was above everything else the Poet of Science. And the general run of exact scientific men have little or nothing to do with poetry ....

His life was the home of fair visions and noble thoughts and courteous, kindly deeds .... I learned to measure many things as but poor and common compared with our friendship.

~ From an account by a Medical Student ~

It was not so much the addresses themselves which told, as the personal intercourse with hundreds of young men to which they formed the introduction. Even his closest friends during those years had only glimpses of the labour, the thought and the anxiety, which it entailed. To deal with a single case he would come through from Glasgow to Edinburgh for an afternoon.

One of his hosts tells me that after having worked all night with men in trouble, he came in to breakfast on Monday morning, fresh and happy as any round the table, and was off to Glasgow before they knew what he had been doing. But there were other times at which the confessions of some of the men and his disappointments with them strained and wore him out.

He has kept letters with strange and awful stories of sin, told for the most part in utter despair. One man writes, 'My past life has been a very wild and sinful one, and I want to know how I am to regard the past. What assurance may I have that the past is forgiven? Do you believe in the Atonement of Christ?'

This letter Drummond 'read to the meeting, and, laying it down, declared his unequivocal faith in the efficacy of Christ's Atonement', and took the opportunity of magnifying the Atonement [which he had been accused of ignoring] as one of the central facts of Christianity. (From a student who was present.)

On another occasion Drummond is reported to have said, 'The sacrifice of Christ is a part of the very essence of Christianity, but the basis of Christianity is the eternal love of God.'

God's forgiveness made sure in Jesus Christ was what he pressed home upon the men whom he found convinced of guilt. Indeed, the secret of his power was his recognition of the enormous variety of religious difficulty and of moral trouble which beset the young men of his time. For every man the thing needful was surrender to Christ, and the beginning of a life of service in His Spirit.

What sheaves of tributes he got, and yet so seldom spoke of them! To quote from two examples:

Some years ago I gave my heart to my Saviour, yet I have not followed him as I ought. But I thank and praise Him that through you I have been enabled by His great unspeakable grace to say, 'Lord, I come'.

I begin to realise how nearly I had become a perfect wreck; in a great measure I owe my escape to your personal influence.

A very strong feature of Drummond's mission was that he recognised that the first duty of his converts was to the University itself and to their studies. In this too, the leaders of the movement set a noble example. Many of them were the first men of their years.

How has it gone since? In nearly every town of our country, in every British colony, in India, in China, in Japan, converts or disciples of this movement, who gratefully trace to it the beginnings of their moral power, are labouring steadfastly, and often brilliantly in every profession of life.

CHAPTER 13

The American Colleges 1887

DRUMMOND, as we have seen, was concentrating his energies upon students. About 1885 Mr Moody too began to specialise in the same direction, and in the spring of 1887 he invited Drummond to a Conference of Students at Northfield, Massachusetts. Drummond agreed to go there, as well as to certain 'summer schools' in Chautauqua and elsewhere.

He might have spent a couple of years, and made a fortune by lecturing. But he saw the opportunity of extending to the American Colleges the religious movement which he had started among the Edinburgh students. He made arrangements for a strong deputation to come over from Edinburgh. He accepted pecuniary engagements only so far as to cover his travelling expenses, and the few purely scientific lectures which he gave were also undertaken by him solely for the purpose of furthering his influence as a religious teacher.

'University Extension' has reached enormous dimensions in the United States [*ie*, in 1898]. Besides the Summer Course at Chicago University, there are the summer schools, to which thousands of people gather at some healthy and beautiful spot (Chautauqua, for instance), to attend regular courses of instruction from experts.

Already I have been asked to become principal of a college, to write for various papers, to lecture in half the States of the Union, and otherwise to line my pocket with dollars. But I have refused all wiles, and am plodding along at Moody's. The hardest thing is the heat. Northfield is like Crieff without the high mountains, but with a larger river and more timber.

After his work at Northfield, Drummond spent a few days at Niagara with Lord and Lady Aberdeen on their way home from India. Then he went to two summer schools.

Imagine 70 acres of forest, with 100 cottages and endless tents buried among the trees, a lake, an orchestra, a vast auditorium, and halls and buildings innumerable. This spot is tenanted for ten days every year by from 3,000 to 6,000 people, who are all busy educating themselves. The vast majority are young men, but there are many old people, entire families, teachers, clergymen, *etc* .... There is much heat here, but no light. The Pharisees are down on one, of course, but the Barbarians show me no little kindness. On the whole, it is a good thing, but a bit of a rabble, and tomorrow I am going to steal away back to Niagara for a quiet Sunday.

~ From a letter to Lady Aberdeen ~

I have lectured today to a vast audience, and am 'on' in half an hour again; subject 'Nature and Religion'. I have been 'interviewed' several times, but some of the accounts are so absurd that I have been ashamed to send them to you.

I never felt so charged with a message. Hundreds of ministers have been coming .... But the people here never seem to have even heard of Christianity.

For two days I have been at a monster hydropathic, 'Clifton Springs'. There are eight resident doctors all the year round and a chaplain .... I could make a fortune here very quickly, but I have other fish to fry. I charged the Chautauqua Company for what science I gave them, and this will cover my expenses. Were it only to break down the universal impression here that all religious work has an equivalent in dollars, I feel it is a duty to enter this small protest.

~ From letters to his Father and Mother ~

I am in correspondence with half the Colleges of America about our work, and my mail-bag is something dreadful.

We have had really splendid work at the Colleges far surpassing our expectations.

~ From letters to Lady Aberdeen ~

At Yale very careful preparation had been made for Drummond's mission. Consequently the work there was very deep, and, in the testimony of many, permanent.

I had a delightful day at Hartford – called on Mark Twain. He is funnier than any of his books, and is a most respected citizen, devoted to things aesthetic, and the friend of the poor and struggling.

Next door to him I found Mrs Harriet Beecher-Stowe – a wonderfully agile old lady, as fresh as a squirrel still, but with a face and air like a lion's. I have not been so taken with anyone on this side of the Atlantic.

I am busy among the medical students of New York, a scattered and lawless set …. Harvard College is *the* college of the country, and under Unitarian auspices, so that I was told it would be impossible to do anything there, but the work was really better than anywhere. I lived with one of the professors, a Unitarian, but I found no difference between him and myself. I have come away with a new idea of the Unitarians, or at least some of them.

After Harvard I spent a couple of days in the American Girton – Wellesley College. It is the largest and most splendid woman's college in the world, and the standard is as high as Harvard. I was the sole male among 600 girl graduates, so you can imagine the terror of the first meetings I had.

★ ★ ★

Three years ago some students in the University of Edinburgh formed an association designed to increase Christian influence and Christian teachings among college men. It has borne fruit. Professor Henry Drummond introduced the same organisation at Yale. The men on the stage last night had come to tell their experiences and tell their fellows here that a man can be a Christian and an athlete and be better for being both ....

The object of such a meeting as this is to counter-balance the false ideas and associations of young men. There has been too much of the bigotry of creed, and not enough practical Christianity in this world.

~ From a report in the New York World *~*

At this meeting, athletes of Yale University described the work of Professor Drummond. One said: 'It was all due to him. He talked to me for an hour one day, and after that I saw my way clear.'

Religion is, in some colleges, becoming more natural. I know of no college in which this change is greater than in Harvard .... The influence of Professor Drummond and his associates has been potent. His youth, his ease of approach, his ability, his simplicity, his method of satisfying the reason before attempting to arouse the feelings or to move the will, appeal with special persuasiveness to college men.

~ From the Boston Congregationalist *~*

There is a marked and growing interest among us in work among the humbler classes of a University Settlement or University Extension kind; and in order to direct this interest wisely, I think I must see what has been done both in England and in Scotland. Pray be sure that a debt of serious obligation is still felt to you here for your wise and inspiring counsel.

~ From a letter from Professor Peabody of Harvard ~

CHAPTER 14

Australia and the Australian Colleges 1890

THERE are always a number of Australians at Edinburgh University, and many of these had been influenced by Professor Drummond's meetings since 1885. In 1889, 230 members of Melbourne University invited him to come out to them. He promised to do so but, faithful to his previous policy, he refused to go among the churches, or do anything that might distract his mission to students, young men and boys. He planned to come home by some of the mission stations in the South Seas and China, and to speak to the students of Japan, who had invited him.

Drummond left London on 14 March 1890.

We have had the most wonderful voyage. There has been no heat to speak of, and one could sail on and on like this for ever .... On Sunday evening I gave an address to about 60 or 70 people – fine young fellows, for the most part, going to push their way in Australia.

I meant to have written you at Colombo, but I found at least four deputations waiting to make life a burden and time a hallucination .... Ceylon itself is worth the whole voyage.

Your prediction was right about the interviewers, who turned up in phalanxes at each port .... A troop of students met me at the pier here [at Melbourne].

Drummond stayed with John Ewing, his fellow-student, his

84

comrade at Sunderland, and one of 'our Club'. In 1887 Ewing was called to the large Presbyterian Church of Toorak, a leading suburb of Melbourne. A week after Drummond landed in Melbourne, Ewing was down with what was thought to be influenza. On the 2nd of May the doctors pronounced it to be typhoid, and on 11 May he passed quietly away.

> He never spoke much, and never said farewell. We had four very happy days together, then the cloud fell, and he was slowly taken from my sight. Oh, Ross, I cannot go on.
>
> ~ *From a letter to D M Ross* ~

> He passed away, my hand in his, more gently than a sleeping child. Strange that I should have been sent across these seas for this.
>
> ~ *From a letter to Lady Aberdeen* ~

> My soul fills with gratitude and enthusiasm for my friend …. He saw always the main stream of the Kingdom of God, all currents in Church or State that make for righteousness, and he threw himself into them.
>
> When he gave us the last Sunday morning's message of his life, you remember he preached on the 'Atonement', and promised to lay before us a further aspect on a future day. Perhaps what he meant to tell us was that the principle of the Atonement was a law of Nature … that up and down the whole of God's creation the one law of life, the supreme condition of progress, the sole hope of the future is Christ's law of the sacrifice of self. If that were his meaning, his sermon has been surely preached.
>
> ~ *From Professor Drummond's address at the Memorial Service* ~

In Melbourne and in Adelaide, Drummond held meetings for students, for young men generally, and for boys and girls. As in Edinburgh he would have nothing but students at his student meetings, and admitted no reporters. Some of the religious papers were very angry at this:

I have been off to Adelaide and put in a week's hard work – meetings, meetings, meetings. I can send you no reports, as I have discovered how to circumvent the Press .... Do not be surprised if you hear that I am off to the South Sea Islands(!) in a few weeks .... France wants the New Hebrides, and Victoria says she shan't get them. They want me to write the thing up at home. Then there is a very crucial missionary problem.

SYDNEY, 7 JUNE:
I arrived in How-d'ye-like-our-Harbour a couple of hours ago .... Melbourne has been one round of meetings .... I never had a night for Government House, but I had every hour of every day filled with what I came to do.

On the way here I had a really happy day in the bush. I saw heaps of kangaroos, dined on the tails thereof, and hunted possums in the moonlight .... I cannot get to Hobart. Time is the culprit. The New Hebrides look nearer. If I go, it will simply take the time I should have given to New Zealand.

We reached a class who never go to church. I should prefer 50 of that class to 1,000 of the church-goers. The great problem in these colonies is the young 'outsider'.

I was told Sydney was the wickedest place in Oceania .... The students have turned out nobly night after night, and they are going to run the meetings henceforth themselves ....

On Sunday I had one of the most curious gatherings I ever faced. Some doctors asked me to address 'the Sydney doctors', of whom it seems only four or so go to church ....

There were exactly 140 present, *all* doctors. I spoke from the standpoint of Evolution, and they were so much interested that next day 20 of them agreed to pay £50 a year each to 'start a church for doctors' on the spot, and get a man out from home at, at least, £1000 a year ....

It is now two in the morning, and in eight hours I start for the New Hebrides. The ship is good, the sea smooth, the cannibals fairly fed at present, and all looks well for a happy voyage.

Drummond's address to [Australian] students must have taken the line of his *Ascent of Man*, for the questions which he kept relate to the reconciliation of the doctrines of evolution with the statements of the Bible as to man's creation. Among the letters he received are a number from men praying for the appearance of a broader and more rational Christianity, and letters which reveal Christian faith wrecked and Christian energies dissipated by the doctrine of verbal inspiration. (In a note to a friend, Drummond declares that this doctrine prevents a man thinking, and castigates 'the paralysing and stunting effect of anything which interferes with the legitimate exercise of human faculty'.) Drummond came across men who still knew only of the older orthodoxy and the easy triumphs which certain infidel writers had obtained over its beliefs in the equal and absolute inspiration of every part of the Bible. And it was no small part of Drummond's mission in Australia, as in Great Britain and America, to bring home the new possibilities of faith which lie in the rational and discriminating criticism of the Old Testament, to which Christ Himself has shown us the way in the Sermon on the Mount.

Wherever Drummond came, men both old and young had new hope, and the weary were refreshed by his sympathy.

CHAPTER 15

Diaries of Travel
3. The New Hebrides

THE New Hebrides lie some 1500 miles east from the coast of Queensland. After long toil and many martyrdoms, the missionaries have civilised the southern islands, the labour traffic has been regulated by the Australian governments, but politically the islands remain, so to speak, in the air, and our Australian colonies resented the claims of France.

It was in order to bear testimony at home on this critical state of affairs that leading men in Australia pressed Drummond to visit the islands. He was also attracted by the prospect of seeing the effects of Christian missions upon a savage people. Moreover, as a geologist, he would have the opportunity of studying islands at once volcanic and of coral formation. On all these lines the bright promise was fulfilled. But, above all, he came home with a new belief in the power of Christianity, and in the heroism of his fellow-churchmen.

[The following are extracts from Drummond's diary]:

The volcano of Tanna very much in evidence all night. Usually a narrow pillar of red, neither dull nor glowing, a red-hot colour, very large, occasionally a brilliant display. This was at a distance of over 40 miles ....

Futuna, one huge block of rock covered completely green ....
On landing all is coral. It extends upwards at least 1000 feet ....
Glorious colour of the sea – bluest blue ....
Ashore on human-back. Small crowd of natives. Some clothed

women, with grass kilts and shell necklaces; huge earrings made of tortoiseshell look like a bunch of keys ....

Dr and Mrs Gunn on this rock for eight years. For six years absolutely no visible result. Now just beginning. New mission-house finely situated on a terrace of coral shrined in palms as usual. Old house destroyed by hurricane lately.

★ ★ ★

Tanna – usual type of Hebrides Island – mountainous, sloping gently toward sea, the belt of tropical vegetation terminating below in the usual fringe of coconut, above in light-green underwood, and wooded to the top ....

Ashore in whale-boat. No sign of life. Then dusky figures gathered, each with his gun, no women or children. Mr Gray stood up, waved hat. Missionary from Wassesi. Magical effect, guns laid down, women came out from the trees. Men helped us ashore ....

The Pure Savage. Men naked with $^3/_4$ inch band of leather or grass. Women with voluminous short skirts in tiers. Some painted red or blue ....

After gentle ascent reached crater, many miles round, with lake in centre, on left the active core rising some 700 or 800 feet higher. Total, 1100 feet ....

Explosions nearly every two or three minutes, like powder in a quarry. At long intervals there were very severe, tremendous explosions without warning, a 'bang', only louder than the loudest thunder, with trembling earth. Superb display of red-hot stones and splashes, shooting to an incredible height, and clattering down in hundreds. Made one spring back, then watch overhead to dodge ....

I saw something like a fountain spouting ....

Very precarious standpoint. But what a spectacle! The fountain resolved itself into a dome of fire of streaming lava, almost white heat, changing immediately into a lurid red, boiling up and exploding every few seconds ....

Descent like coming down a snow mountain on the Alps. Had

to put up sun umbrellas to shield ourselves from the volcanic dust ....

Came to a native village, first a magnificent Platz – oval sward surrounded with spreading banyan-trees, where dances and feasts are held. Then reed-cane fence. Women came out, dogs barked, children trooped round. No men. Where? Away drinking kava, *ie* 'at the public house'.

★ ★ ★

Went off to island, Fila, for service. Mr and Mrs Michelsen tried to Christianise this some years ago. No success. Now the whole island is Christian, an out-station of Mr Mackenzie. I spoke 20 minutes, 2 Cor. iii:18. Mr Macdonald translated afterwards.

Very attentive .... Charming spot .... Heathenism will soon be forgotten.

★ ★ ★

Earthquakes very frequent in all the islands. On Tongoa counted seventeen in one day. Can see the banyan-trees twisting and shaking.

★ ★ ★

[On Tongoa] great assemblage of natives on beach, red cloth predominating; very picturesque; fires smoking. Every man different .... One handsome damsel in red gown picking her teeth vigorously with a carving-knife, rim of strawberry basket on head, one or two wild-flowers stuck in it ....

Most men have shirts and a loin cloth, red, over them. Women have either skirts of calico, spotted and striped, or a nightgown.

Remarkable variety of foliage on all islands, but especially here. Every shade of green, wooded to the top of highest hill. Natives very kind and quiet, in spite of the butcher's knife most of them carry .... House 400 feet; grand view of sea and island. Mr Michelsen's station a model of neatness. Trim, terraced garden, glowing with balsam, roses, and golden egg-plant. Most unassuming of men, simple Norwegian ....

Mr M. has been 11 years in Tongoa. All Christian. Three years ago the last cannibal feast. Was introduced to a man who had been at it, the 'pièce de résistance' being his own half-brother ....

On Tongoa natives are very well off. Far better than the Africans. Better off than the crofters in the Highlands.

★ ★ ★

Planting new station for Mr Smaill [on Api]. To land, wade over coral-reef with shoes on, delicate branches, antlers, cauliflower, almost sacrilege to walk on them ....

Poor Mrs Smaill, what a home! .... Lunch on beach. Awful crowd of savages surrounded us as we ate. Every man stark naked, except for infinitesimal strip between legs, turned into a belt of bark. Women wear a scant loin-cloth of bark.

All armed, mostly rifles, cocked .... Immense curiosity as each article was carried ashore. Cane deck chair very exciting; use undreamt of till I sat down in it amid great laughter.

★ ★ ★

Volcano of Lofevi a superb cone of great grace rising out of the sea ....

Confab on beach. 'Now Missi come; no more war, all change now. Sing-song tomorrow, kill pig, dance.' Celebrate the end of heathenism, and arrival of missionary. One thing they all know, that when he comes there is peace ....

Many murders on this beach and cannibal feasts. Land next year, and probably there will not be a weapon on the shore.

★ ★ ★

Plenty of rain; safely 100 inches per annum. Never flood, never drought, the rainfall is so distributed ....

First year make a nursery of coffee plants. In three years you have your first crop. There is no disease; no manure is needed. Almost the sole risk is a hurricane ....

Fever not serious anywhere, and most islands quite free from it ....

Natives have often professed to sell land as theirs; when the real owner turns up, a row is inevitable. Some of the missionaries have paid for their land to one 'owner' after another ....

English skies in New Hebrides, not blistering, burnished skies. White clouds as at home, and even dull days ....

Corals individually are exquisite, but do not expect to see them like what they are in Kensington. Shells ditto.

★ ★ ★

All trade is done in pigeon-English. French labour boats have to use it.

★ ★ ★

Missionary settles in a village often by request of natives. Either (1) they want a 'missi', as he will see justice done between them and passing trader: he is known as always on the side of the natives; (2) the islanders may have shot so many boats' crews, that they want him as a guarantee of good behaviour; (3) labour men returned may have been influenced in Queensland and want a teacher; or (4) they know that Christianity will abolish sorcery, which is the cause of all death and war. They *do* want to stop war, and therefore ask missionary. Christianised natives never carry firearms.

Having seen one end of the labour traffic in the New Hebrides, Drummond went on a tour in Queensland to find out about the other. He not only investigated the facts about the importation of the Kanakas to the sugar plantations, but inquired as well into the condition of the Queensland Aborigines.

The question of continuing the labour traffic with Polynesia is an anthropological rather than an economic question. They are utterly uncivilised except in the few cases where the patient labours of the missionaries have had some civilising and softening influence.

They know nothing of the outside world .... The Kanaka is easily persuaded to engage to accompany the trader for a term of years, when a few sticks of tobacco, a gun, or some other toy is put into his hands as a present ....

On the island of Eromanga, the first missionary was murdered, and several after him. But now the missionary whom I found there has been at his post for 13 years, and the Kanakas live peacefully together. Can you wonder at the missionaries protesting when the pick of their young men have gone to the sugar plantations in Queensland? ....

The drafting of natives to a civilised country and then shipping them back again might become an important factor in the progress of these races. Everything would depend on the treatment they received and the moral atmosphere which surrounded them. The Queensland Government has certainly left no stone unturned to secure that the Kanakas are safe on Australian soil from any possible tyranny, violence, or even physical discomfort ....

Though Kanaka labour is far too costly to be trifled with, it is questionable whether they gain anything either morally or materially. Their hard-earned wages they cannot take back in coin, since money is almost unknown in Polynesia. What they do take back is usually a lot of rubbish, purchased in Brisbane at fancy prices ....

It is impossible not to compare the action of the Queensland Government, where the Kanakas are concerned, with their treatment of their own natives, who are treated as veritable outcasts. They are driven away from the towns and settlements, and their lives in certain districts are freely taken on the smallest provocation, and no questions asked.

~ From an interview in the Pall Mall Gazette *~*

From Australia, Drummond voyaged slowly by Java to Singapore and Saigon, and came round to Hong Kong and Shanghai.

Among the South Sea Islands I saw men who ten years ago were cannibals; why not now? Because the missionaries of Jesus Christ have been among them; and these people gave me their spears and bows – 'because,' they said, 'we do not need them any more' ....

If we learn from Christ, we shall be made light and salt and leaven to those among whom we dwell.

~ From an address given at Shanghai ~

From China he went on to Japan, and at Tokyo was able to answer the invitation sent him a year before by a large number of students. He addressed about 500 of them. From Japan he came home through Canada.

In November 1890 he opened the College Session with an address upon Missions, [extracts from which follow]:

One view is that the world is lost, and must be saved; the other, that the world is sunken, and must be raised .... The first is the standpoint of the popular evangelism, the second is the view of evolution. I add to the watchword 'Evolution' the qualifying term 'Christian'. This alone takes account of the whole nature of man, of sin and guilt, of the future and of the past, and recognises the Christian facts and forces as alone adequate to deal with them ....

★　★　★

It is irrational for the missionary to carry the same *form* of message to every land .... When he reaches his field, his duty is to find out what God has sown there already, for there is no field in this world where the Great Husbandman has not sown something ....

In Australia the chief problem of Christianity is that it may be wholly ignored in the pressure of competing growths.

The South Sea Islands lie at the opposite end of the scale. These people are the amoebae of the human world ....

China stands midway between, an instance of arrested development. On the fair way to become a vertebrate, it has stopped short at

the crustacean. There is a powerful religion already in possession.

Japan is an almost perfect contrast to China. It is the insect imerging from the chrysalis. Its own religion was abandoned a few years ago, and the country is looking for another ....

Missionary staff should be differentiated with more exactness than at present. Each man would make his choice and become a specialist ....

The reason why more of the best men do not go to the foreign field is uncertainty as to whether the cut of their theology quite qualifies them .... I am not arguing for free-lances, or budding sceptics, or rationalists being turned loose on our mission-fields, but for young men who combine with all modern culture the consecrated spirit and Christ-like life ....

We require a further class, not wholly absorbed with the inculcation of Western Creeds, but whose outlook goes forth to the nation as a whole – men who will help on its education, its morality, and its healthy progress in all that makes for righteousness. This man places the accent, not on the progress of a church, but on the coming of the Kingdom of God ....

The mission in the New Hebrides cannot attract this class of minds. It is a mission of pure benevolence. But the missionaries themselves do not ask for more workers there.

In China small congregations are springing up everywhere, but they possess no common programme, and the educated classes are not being reached ....

It is the opinion of many men who know China intimately that half of the preaching is absolutely useless. The warning ought at least to be heard. The call is frequently uttered with a harrowing importunity and sensationalism of appeal, which makes it seem blasphemy to decline. The kind of missionary secured by this process is neither the wisest nor the best; and China not only needs to be protected from these men, but they need to be protected from themselves and from those who appeal to them ....

Japan is the most interesting country in the world at this moment. The Japanese have set themselves up with all the materials of an advanced and rising civilised state except one. They are in the unique position of prospecting for a religion ....

There are already thousands of Christian converts, very many as cultured as the picked men in our universities!

A leader of thought among these said to me, 'We found that Christianity was a greater and a richer thing than the missionaries had told us .... We want Christianity, not perhaps necessarily Western Christianity .... '

A Japanese Christian pastor told me, 'Tell them that we want them to send us no more doctrines. Japan wants Christ'. The immediate outlook seems to me one of the richest promise.

★ ★ ★

On the whole mission-field he had visited, Drummond said, 'If one saw a single navvy trying to remove a mountain, the desolation of the situation would be appalling; but when one sees Christians working by the thousand in every land, the majesty of the missionary work fills and inspires the mind'.

CHAPTER 16

1891-1894

WE have seen with what admiration the missionaries inspired Drummond. He once said that their life helped him to understand the Incarnation. Yet his critics fastened upon those portions of the College address summarised at the end of the last chapter in which he stated the still unsolved problems of the mission-field. But the astonishing thing is that Christian men should base such charges upon a necessarily brief report in a newspaper. It is still more grievous that, when this has been pointed out to them, they should not express regret at having misrepresented a fellow-Christian. Drummond's letters of this date are full of pain, and, for the first time in his life, of warm indignation on his own behalf. He calls his traducers 'assassins of character'.

His uncle wrote him a very kind letter, expressing his disappointment at finding that 'you all but ignore the Atonement'. To this Drummond replied:

A man's only right to publish an address is that he thinks the thing said there is not being said otherwise. Now, ninety per cent of the evangelical literature of the day is expressly devoted to enforcing what I am accused of not enforcing, *ie* the fundamentals of Christianity. Of course you may think I make an error of judgement .... But there seem to me very many more books on those aspects of Christ's work than on the others, and I must give the message that *in addition* seems to me to be needed.'

[In 1892, in a later letter to Mr Sankey, then in Scotland, Drummond wrote]:

Would that all calling themselves by the sacred name of Christian had your charity; knew the meaning, as you and Mr Moody do, of 'judge not', and afforded a man at least a frank trial before convicting him ....

My message lies among the forgotten truths, the false emphasis, and the wrong accent. To every man his work.

The way to make souls hard and bitter and revengeful is to treat them as many treat me. If I have escaped this terrible fate, it is because there are others like yourself who 'think no evil'.

The session of 1890-91 was spent in his college work, his weekly visits to the Edinburgh students, and a multitude of other duties. In April came a call to the sick-bed of his friend Robert Barbour, who had been carried to the Riviera. This vigil lasted for three weeks. He read, cheered and tended the dying man. Barbour died on 27 May.

Barbour's peculiar characteristic was saintliness, an element in life which is after all a vital ingredient. It is the unworldly people who have really helped us most.

~ From a letter to Lord Aberdeen ~

Perhaps this is the most convenient point at which to describe the place Drummond took in the life of Glasgow. From 1885 he lived in No 3 Park Circus, above the West End Park. He could not use the whole of it, but he worked best when there was space about him, and the house afforded a noble study, with a long view northwards across some suburbs to the Campsie Hills.

Till the end he added to his store of beautiful cabinets, and of pictures of which accuracy obliges me to say that they were of more or less ambiguous value. The hall had a few spoils of travel. The study contained a large library, scientific, theological and literary.

At the writing-table against one of the windows Drummond wrote only letters. All his other work was done in a chair with his back to the light, and a large blotter on his knee.

His working day began after an 8.30 breakfast. He read or wrote till his lecture at 12, lunched at one, and generally went out to walk or to business till 4.30 or 5. After tea he settled down, if he was permitted, to a long spell of work till 10. But his evenings were often broken by visitors. Men came to consult him about Liberal prospects. On behalf of philanthropic societies he was constantly receiving visitors. But in addition there drifted upon him all sorts of individuals, representing only themselves. Yet even their visits, frequent and prolonged as they could be, were exceeded by the letters which came in showers. It was impossible for him to overtake even that portion which had a real claim on his attention. He had no staff of clerks, nor a secretary.

The summer of 1892 brought another General Election. Drummond took a smaller part in it than in the previous one.

During September he took a fishing at Banchory-Ternan, on the Dee. Then, and for the rest of the autumn, he was hard at work on *The Ascent of Man*.

In November I joined the Glasgow College, and lived for the first month of the session with Drummond. It was then I became aware of the big correspondence and large number of daily visits to which he was subject, and learned to admire his constant patience, and the leisure he made for those who had the least claim upon him.

It has been commonly supposed that he hung loose to church life, and very seldom of a Sunday worshipped with his fellow-Christians. I can only say that during all the winters I worked by his side in Glasgow, I never knew him to miss attending church on Sunday; and a more hearty and reverent worshipper it would be hard to find.

He very seldom went to a party, but he made an exception for the social meetings of students. There his gaiety was always infectious. On Saturday afternoons he was always found watching football.

By the end of the session of 1892-93 he had written his lectures on *The Ascent of Man,* and on 22 March sailed on the 'Teutonic' for America.

In Boston, the Lowell Institute Lectures of 1893 aroused the most vivid interest. They were practically his volume on *The Ascent of Man.* 'For every one who received a ticket of admission to them, there were ten turned away' (Editor of the *Boston Congregationalist*).

Drummond repeated the lectures. But the strain of this not-withstanding, he gave addresses to the students of Harvard University. One of these concluded with the characteristic words: 'Above all things, do not touch Christianity unless you are willing to seek the kingdom of heaven first. I promise you a miserable existence if you seek it second.'

In July he repeated his Boston lectures at Chautauqua, and went on to a Conference, under Mr Moody, at Northfield. Here he delivered three addresses. The reporter of one of the leading English religious papers said to him that he had orders not to report a word of what Drummond said; and a deputation urged Mr Moody not to allow Drummond to speak. Mr Moody informed them that he was to go on – being the man who once said to the writer of this volume, 'There's nothing I ever read of Henry Drummond's, or heard him say, that I didn't agree with'. Drummond wrote some days afterwards:

At Northfield I felt a great deal out of it, and many fell upon me and rent me. Before the close of the Conference, I struck an orthodox vein and retrieved myself a little. But it was not a happy time.

In the end of July he went on holiday into Canada. In the first week of October he was back in Chicago for the opening of the University. He often said how large and open he found life to be there, and how strongly it roused the best that was in him. Outside the University was the Great Exposition, about whose beauty and vastness he could hardly cease talking when he came home. Drummond addressed the Congress of the Evangelical Alliance.

It is astonishing how his words touched the hearts of American men and women, who, brought up to religion, had suddenly found it mere routine, and had slipped away from faith. At the risk of offending the orthodox, he adapted his teaching to such cases; he knew that these existed in crowds, unsought, uncared for. Physically, this visit to America tired him greatly, and he came home looking much older.

The winter session of 1893-94 was passed in work harder than usual. He was preparing his Boston discourses for the press. He gave a number of lectures outside the College, and on 5 February began his last series of addresses to the Edinburgh students. About this time he was offered the Principalship of McGill University, Montreal, and he did not refuse it till after long consideration.

In May *The Ascent of Man* was published.

CHAPTER 17

The Ascent of Man

DRUMMOND looked forward to a long revision of his Lowell Lectures. Before he left America, however, he heard that a Philadelphian publisher was about to issue a volume entitled '*The Evolution of Man,* being the Lowell Lectures delivered … by Professor Henry Drummond'.

The case was carried into Court. In pronouncing judgement, Judge Dallas remarked that:

> The defendant, while precisely adopting his title from the headlines of the report [in the *British Weekly*], has so altered the text as to make it appear that what his book contains is the precise language of the author of the lectures, although it contains only some of the lectures, and presents none of them fully or correctly.

The edition – 10,000 copies, with the stereotype plates – was ordered to be destroyed, and Drummond got his costs.

But Drummond was obliged to hasten his own publication of the lectures, and after being able, to his chagrin, to spend only the leisure of one busy winter in revising them, he sent them to press in the spring of 1894, and they were published in May of that year.

The Ascent of Man was looked for with the interest and the curiosity which await the works only of the most popular writers. The author could not have expected so unanimous a chorus of praise as had greeted the appearance of his *Natural Law.* The reports of his lectures had already excited the suspicion of some and the full-armed hostility of others. On the whole, the criticism of the reviewers when it came was worthy and without ulterior motives. The fairness of his reviewers Drummond himself heartily acknowledged.

The book had all the external qualities of his previous works – the lucid style, the power and charm of illustration, and the many happy phrases. It disarmed too a large number of the most severe critics of *Natural Law*. In the latter Drummond had attempted to carry physical processes into the region of the moral and the spiritual; in *The Ascent of Man* he essayed the converse task, and succeeded in showing the ethical at work in regions of life generally supposed to be given over to purely physical laws.

In *Natural Law* Drummond had said that in the feelings and the reason of the natural man there was nothing of grace nor the power of the Spirit. He had in fact excommunicated Nature, and, without intending it, had given his support to a dualism which emphasises the opposition between human reason and either revelation, or grace, or religious authority. Between 1883 and 1893 Drummond had recognised the falseness of this dualism, and he states in *The Ascent of Man:*

> Nothing can ever be gained by setting one half of Nature against the other, or the rational against the ultra-rational. To affirm that Altruism is a peculiar product of religion is to excommunicate Nature from the moral order, and religion from the rational order.

And again:

> If Nature is the Garment of God, it is woven without a seam throughout .... For to break up Nature is to break up Reason, and with it God and Man.

For such a recantation *The Ascent of Man* received a warm welcome from the most severe of the philosophic critics of its predecessor. Nor was it in this respect any less welcome to the theologian. For the book vindicated Nature, as also the sphere of the God of Love, and sought to prove the presence of the characteristic forces of Christianity – sympathy and self-sacrifice upon the lower stages of the evolution of man.

The book covers the evolution of man both as an animal, a rational being, and a member of society. It draws its proofs and illustrations from biology, the sciences of language and of the origin of mind, as well as from modern research into the beginnings of the human family. In all these departments Drummond made use of the thoughts of many thinkers.

He has certainly expounded the appearances of Altruism, which are present in the earlier stages of evolution, as these had never been illustrated or impressed upon the public mind by any previous writer. Drummond draws a distinction between 'The Struggle for Life' and 'The Struggle for the Life of Others', and makes the charge against Charles Darwin of omitting all notice of the latter. But Mr George Carr [an Agnostic] points out that, when Darwin spoke of the 'struggle for life', he had in view the struggle of the species.

The Ascent of Man was charged with containing a number of errors in the domain of physical science.

Professor Macalister (Anatomy, Cambridge): 'Once or twice his love for analogy betrays [the author] into trivial misconceptions.' It cannot be denied that there are some grounds for the charges of hasty inference and exaggeration of emphasis on certain points which seem favourable to the author's main thesis.

Professor Macalister: 'In its origination cell division is really selfish, and solely for self-interest, as far as this language of moral import can be applied to a biological process.'

Similarly Professor McKendrick (Physiology, Glasgow), who adds: 'One cannot help feeling that in not a few of the illustrations Professor Drummond reads into the phenomena of nature some of his own mental moods.'

Professor Iverach, in a review which called forth from Drummond a warm acknowledgement of its justice, pointed out that the argument of the book avoided such difficult questions as are raised 'by the stumbling and the failures of evolution, and the persistency of lower forms of life alongside the higher'.

In answer to this, it might be urged that the book is the work of a poetic translator of the science of his time, rather than of an original scientific thinker. Still, if this were granted, others might justly urge that Drummond sinned also in art, by overdoing his case.

It would not be fair to give these adverse criticisms without adding from the same critics their appreciation of the volume as a whole.

Professor Macalister: 'It is an honest and manly attempt to grapple in a reverential spirit with these difficulties.'

Professor McKendrick: 'The Introduction ... emphasises the contribution that the author has added to the discussion, namely, the recognition of the great principle of the "struggle for others" as a factor in Evolution. It has never been put forward with such force and fullness as by Professor Drummond .... This is the portion of the book that will awake thought in many minds, and lead them to look again at Nature ....

'A thorough-going evolutionary view demands a new theology .... Professor Drummond deserves credit for the clear-sightedness with which he sees that all must be ultimately explained by the application of one great Law or Principle representing the Mind of God working out the Harmony of His Universe.'

In addition, Professor Gairdner (Medicine, Glasgow): 'Nothing that I have read on the subject of ethical theory has appeared to me to go so deep or to be so convincing as this, which makes [altruism] a fundamental part of God's universe from the beginnings.'

Finally, from a philosophical standpoint, Revd D M Ross, one of Drummond's closest friends, whose criticism of the main thesis of *Natural Law* had been adverse:

The Ascent of Man is unquestionably his greatest book. The chief interest is not in its proofs, but in what it seeks to prove – that love, or the struggle for the life of others, is a law deeply embedded in the whole life of the universe .... [Drummond writes] 'Evolution is not progress in matter. Matter cannot progress. It is a progress in spirit, in that which is at once most human, most rational, most divine .... Evolution is revelation, the progressive realisation of the ideal, the ascent of Love' .... Had he lived to follow out these hints contained in the last chapter of *The Ascent of Man*, he had it in him to do work as an Evangelist to the scientific and cultured classes for which the great work he had already done would have seemed but a preparation.

CHAPTER 18

The Boys' Brigade

HENRY Drummond had climbed to the height of experience and success; he was on familiar terms with the greatest of men of his generation; but some angel had blessed him with the fortunate gift of still being able to look out on life from the level of a boy's eyes.

He read a boy's heart, and knew on what side religion touched him. Lads who shirked religious meetings did not shirk those which Drummond held. His addresses had nothing about them of the conventional or condescending – the 'my-dear-young-friends' attitude. In substance they were true to his maxim that 'a boy's religion must be his own, and ought not to be his grandmother's or his aunt's'. How happy he was with boys, and what trouble he took to be kind to them.

To some boys in 1889 he sent 'examination papers'. Here are some of the questions:

HISTORY:
- Where was Major Whittle born; contrast him briefly with Wellington, Napoleon, General Booth, General Tom Thumb, and General Supply Stores.
- Are you a Home-Ruler: if so, why not?

DOMESTIC ECONOMY:
- Name the two best brands of shortbread. What is long-bread, and how does it differ from high-bred?

– How would you spend 2d if you got it? Subtract $\frac{1}{2}$d from 2d, and
parse the remainder.

PHYSIOLOGY:
– 'Define the term 'Get-your-hair-cut', and say if red hair is hair-red-itary.
– Where was your face before it was washed?

In Glasgow, message and telegraph boys, the urchins that play
football behind the policeman's back, and the little ragamuffin
bands which used some years ago to parade the streets with penny
whistles and tin pails – these were his constant entertainment.

Some years ago it was not uncommon for boys and girls to be
sent from shops with baskets or parcels far too heavy for them. In
some cases, the constant carriage of a heavy basket on the elbow
drew round the shoulder-blade and rendered the child slightly
deformed for life. Drummond had baskets made to strap over the
shoulders and rest on the back like a knapsack. Several tradesmen
in Glasgow adopted these.

But the moral problem of the city-boy was a much harder one.
In many Sunday-schools the discipline was genuine; and here
and there, teachers of rough boys kept in touch with them
through the rest of the week. But in a very large proportion of
Sunday-schools discipline was fitful, and the teachers did nothing
to control the life of their pupils. The crisis was becoming des-
perate, for a large number of teachers annually deserted a work
of which they recognised the futility and for which they knew
of no other methods.

Mr W A Smith was a Glasgow merchant and a Sunday-school
teacher. On 4 October 1883 he formed 30 of the pupils of his own
school into a company, and tried upon them the effects of regular
drill. This was the first company of the now famous Boys' Brigade.
The movement rapidly spread, in connection with nearly every
branch of the Christian Church.

The distinguishing feature of the organisation is that it has two
sides – the military and religious – which are not separate, but

closely interwoven. But the deeper and the principal operations of the movement are upon the religious side.

From the first, the movement secured Henry Drummond's hearty and deliberate co-operation. He was consulted by its promoters, entered its councils, frequently addressed its members, wrote books for them, and pled for them before the public. Next to his own work among the Edinburgh students, there was no institution of our time to which he gave more thought in the last ten years of his life.

The boy is accounted for by the Evolution Theory. His father was the Primitive Man. It is only his being in a town and his mispronunciation that make you think he is not a savage. What he represents is Capacity; he is clay, dough, putty. He is simply Boy, pure, unwashed, unregenerate Boy. Until the 'BB' was discovered, scarcely any one knew how to make a man, a gentleman, and a Christian out of a message-boy ....

Let us suppose you have gathered a Sunday-class of boys, and treat them at first on the old or time-dishonoured plan. Infinite trouble and infinite bribery have brought these creatures together; and as they come solely to amuse themselves, your whole effort is spent in keeping order – in quelling riots, subduing irrelevant remarks, minimising attacks upon the person. No boy, you know perfectly, has yet succeeded in listening to you for two consecutive minutes. They have learned nothing whatever. Respect is unknown, obedience a jest.

What is wrong is that they have no motive, no interest, and you have not tried to find these for them ....

One night, after the usual émeute, you retire from the place of torture, vowing to attempt some change. The following Saturday night, instead of trying to find out whether the Israelites crossed the Red Sea by the shoals at Suez or went round, 'as some say', by Wady Tawarik, you read up the literature of the 'BB', and learn how the children of your own city can be led across the more difficult sea of life's temptations ....

Call these boys 'boys', which they are, and ask them to sit up in a Sunday-class, and no power on earth will make them do it, but put a fivepenny cap on them and call them 'soldiers', which they are not, and you can order them about till midnight .... As class, it was confusion, depression, demoralisation, chaos. As Company, it is respect, self-respect, enthusiasm, happiness, peace.

~ *From an article in* Good Words ~

Drummond states that the Brigade takes boys between 12 and 17, being 'designed to operate on a boy only during a specific part of his development', and then hand him over to the YMCA, or Church Guilds, or the like.

Then follows emphasis on the fact that every Company must be connected with a Church, Mission, or other Christian organisation.

It cannot be stated too emphatically that the Boys' Brigade is a religious movement. Everything is subsidiary to this idea .... The emphasis upon the manly, rather than the mawkish, presentation of Christianity has been its stronghold from the first ....

The military organisation is but an aid, and this fact is continually kept before the officers .... That the war-spirit exists at all among the boys of any single Company would certainly be news to the officers, and if it did arise it would as certainly be checked ....

In addition to Sunday-classes, nearly every Company reports an address given at drill on the week-night; and each parade is opened and closed with a prayer, or with a short religious service ....

It is clear that, in dealing with boys, supreme importance must be attached to maintaining a right attitude towards athletics. The Captains are not so much above the boys in years as to have lost either their love or knowledge of sports. The wise officer, the humane and sensible officer, in short makes as much use of play for higher purposes as of the parades, and possibly more ....

The good officer is not only the boys' guide, philosopher, and friend, but their brother. In distress, in sickness, they can count upon him .... He is Pastor of Boys; and, if he is the right man, of their homes ....

Many of the prime movers in this new cause are men who have been almost strangers to such work before. But they saw here something definite, practical, human, which could give them a useful life-interest outside themselves ....

There is probably nothing open just now to laymen which has in it anything like the same substance and promise as this.

CHAPTER 19

The End

THE first touches of the disease which ultimately killed him were felt by Drummond in the spring of 1894 – on the back of a winter of hard work. He had an easy summer, but, when he returned to college in November, his face looked worn, and he would shield himself from cold in a way we had never seen him do before. In December he had sharp attacks of sickness, but he held to his college work without complaint, and even arranged for the opening of a new line of work.

This was the establishment of a 'Pleasant Sunday Afternoon' for the men of that district of Glasgow known as Port Dundas.

Drummond had at first an exaggerated idea of the dislike of the men, for whom the meetings were planned, to the forms of religion, and he intended that there should be almost no prayers. This idea, however, was abandoned. Drummond grew too ill to take his promised share of the work, but till the last his heart was in it. I do not think he sufficiently realised the danger of leading men away from the family aspects of religion, yet the meetings attracted a large number of men who would otherwise not have attended a religious service.

He intended to go to Edinburgh as usual for some of the student meetings in February and March. But at last he had to write to Professor Simpson: 'I see now the inevitable must be faced. I have had a second breakdown in health since Christmas, and .... I feel it would be wrong to attempt Edinburgh in my present condition.'

It was grievous to watch him at the work to which he clung in spite of all his pain and our remonstrances. The straight, lithe figure, which used to bring brightness into our sombre college, crossed the vestibule bent and stiff. We found he was not sleeping at night, and his face grew pinched. So he struggled on till just a few days before the end of the session, when his doctors peremptorily forbade more lectures.

For change of air and relief from the constant siege of interests which his house endured, he left Glasgow – left it for the last time. His work was done.

His disease, though this was not known till afterwards, was produced by a malignant growth of the bones, that caused him intense agony. As the months passed, it deprived him of all power to move, and made him brittle. Except for some moments during the last weeks, his mind was unclouded. He retained unabated the vigour, and even the brilliance, of his intellect. His sense of humour never left him, and his room became a kind of 'pool' for new stories. He greeted you in his old way with a flash of welcome, had a score of questions to ask about your work, chaffed you, and chaffed himself too.

No man had such friends or more devoted physicians. Some of the former, and his brother, were always within hail of him; the latter gave weeks out of their busy lives to watch beside his bed. And so he sank slowly down a long slope.

He was taken to Edinburgh in March 1895, [then to the south of France, the hot baths at Dax, Biarritz, and London, then] to Tunbridge Wells, where he lay under the care of an old friend, Dr Claude Wilson. He remained there till the end. At first he was able to go about in a bath chair, and even to walk a few steps in the open air. But as winter came on, he moved only between his bed and the dining-room. Soon he ceased to sit up, and his couch was wheeled from the one room to the other.

Twice or thrice he said, 'I have been giving all my life, and now it seems to me positively indecent to be only getting'. Every good work of which he heard still roused his interest, and sometimes he longed to be up again for his share in it.

He was not without hopes of recovery, but it was always diffi-cult to know whether he really felt these, or uttered them for our sakes. Yet from August 1896 his general health improved, he put on flesh. The cessation of pain was due to the progress of the dis-ease, and only showed how nearly this had finished its work.

On Sunday, 7 March, Dr [Hugh] Barbour played to him some hymn tunes, then he tried the old Scots melody of 'Martyrdom', to which Drummond beat time with his hand, and joined in the words 'I'm not ashamed to own my Lord'. When the hymn was done, he said, 'There's nothing to beat that, Hugh'.

His mind wandered upon old themes. He talked, half dreaming, about John's Gospel. On Thursday morning he murmured a mes-sage to his mother, became unconscious, and passed away very quietly about 11 o' clock.

Upon the following Monday, we went to Stirling to lay his body beside his father's, on the Castle Rock, in the shadow of the old Greyfriars' Church. This was not the only mourning for him. Services were held in many towns of the kingdom; also in Princeton University, at Ottawa, at Adelaide, at Singapore, and I know not where else. Yet at Stirling it seemed as if all were represented. There gathered mourners from every stage of his life: his own people, the magistrates of the town, his mates at school and college, his fellow-workers in every cause for which he laboured; but chiefly a crowd of young men, students in Edinburgh and Glasgow, yet from all parts of the Empire, and from lands beyond, whose fresh faces shone with the bright assurance that Henry Drummond's work on earth would not cease.

Index